TIME BANDITS

THE MOVIE SCRIPT

WRITTEN BY

TERRY GILLIAM AND MICHAEL PALIN

OF

MONTY PYTHON

Dolphin Books
Doubleday & Company, Inc.
Garden City, New York
1981

ISBN: 0-385-17732-1
Library of Congress Catalog Card Number 81-43117
Dolphin Books
Doubleday & Company, Inc.

Printed in the United States of America

Who are the TIME BANDITS

where do they come from and how much do they cost ? These are some of the still unsolved questions. Who or what are these creatures - timeless, yet always late; immortal, yet destructible; capable of inter-galactic, inter-cosmic travel, yet unable to tie their own shoelaces ?

All that is known for certain is that they helped God create the world. First in the Trees and Small Shrubs Department, then, after the unfortunate creation of The Pink BunkadooTree, in the lowly-paid recesses of the Repairs Department, (putting fins back on dolphins, repainting rainbows etc.). After this the history of the Time Bandits is less clear, but they appear to have been given the job of cataloguing and re-sealing small holes which had appeared in Time and Space (both of which God had rushed through late on a Friday). Then they vanished. No-one, least of all The Supreme Being (to give God his full name) would have worried except that it was discovered that they had taken with them the priceless map of the time-holes.

With their re-appearance millions of years later in an English schoolboy's bedroom they began brief but wild careers Time Bandits. Chased by The Supreme Being in and out of ten centuries, and lured on to near-death and near disaster by the forces of Evil, they were only saved by a hairsbreadth from totally destroying themselves and the world.

After this they disappeared back to Creation and have not been heard of since.

But they could re-appear at any moment, so for those of you who may hear strange rumblings coming from their bedroom cupboard at the dead of night, here is something that may help…

A Spotter's Guide

Randall

Self-styled leader of the Time Bandits. The only man strong enough to keep together a gang who are determined not to have a leader.
Randall was mostly born 624,000 years ago, somewhere in Hyper-space (possibly Trenton, Andromeda). Studied Elementary Creation and Universe Planning. Helped create Earth, but most designs rejected - e.g. singing amoeba, covers (to stop volcanoes getting dirty) mountains which slope only one way, barking sheep. Intensely competitive, Randall modelled himself on the Supreme Being, but ran out of modelling clay.
Ambition: To be able to spell "dynasty".
Favourite Colour: Black spots.

Strutter

Also known as Schtrutter, Strotter or John Diefenbaker (rarely), Strutter is an expert on indecision. If ever anything has to be seen from both sides without either one appearing to offer a totally satisfactory course of action, Strutter (or Schtrutter) is your man. Anywhere in the world, at any time of day or night Strutter stands ready to be not sure quite what to do. Among his many magic powers is the ability to transfer his thoughts to chickens; to make hot tea go cold; and to spell "dynasty".
Favourite Colour: Green or blue, or possibly yellow..though red's nice...no..no brown ! Definitely brown. Or grey.

Og

Life as we know it was not believed to exist on Og, but a probe which passed within 70,000 miles of his surface detected tiny thought particles being emitted from the heavy gaseous mass known as his head, which it was thought, would coalesce over a period of thousands of years to form an "idea". This eventually happened,. But it was a rotten idea. Called the Pink Bunkadoo, it was a tree 600 feet tall, bright pink, with a frightful smell. For this the Supreme Being took Og and his friends off a good steady job in Trees and down to the Repairs Department (which is where the Great Adventure began)
Ambition: To find out what "ambition" means.
Favourite Colour: The one with red in it.
Favourite Rock Group: Devonian Sandstone

to the Time Bandits

Wally

Known to his friends as "Wally", Wally is a keep-fit fanatic. He can run faster, jump higher and sing louder than any of the others, provided he's frightened enough. He comes from a long line of Wallys in the tree designing business - in fact he spent many years as part of a tree himself, before branching off into other things. Struck by a meteor shower when he was quite young, Wally lost his memory and for a while believed he was handsome, intelligent and fearless. He met Randall whilst working on a brand new evergreen tree, which kept falling to one side. It was called the lurch. He's also generally held responsible for the now extinct camel, otter and haddock trees.
Ambition: To rule the world (except on Thursday afternoons and weekends).
Favourite Colour: Money
Favourite Friend: Fidgit

Fidgit

Born several times over the last trillion years, Fidgit was an early galaxy creator. He and his team worked on plans for the first Black Holes, but they always fell through. Amongst many other strange powers Fidgit has an uncanny knack of knowing exactly what people are going to say long after they've said it. His strange hat was a present from his workmates to celebrate his billionth birthday. It was supposed to be an iron mask, but the bottom fell off.
Fidgit has the highest I.Q. of all the Time Bandits, ·013.
Ambition: Pluto
Favourite Food: To be asked the name of his favourite planet.
Favourite Planet: Beans

Vermin

A compulsive eater. Born "Muhammed Ali" he changed his name to Vermin to get work. His extraordinary eating habits came to light when a couple of small galaxies were found to be missing. In the nick of time the Supreme Being slapped Vermin hard on the back, causing pieces of half-digested planet to fly off into space, where they eventually cooled and formed the Solar System (the Big Burp theory). Vermin has the only digestive system ever to win a Nobel Prize.
Ambition: To drool the world
Favourite Food: Wood, concrete, papiermaché, tin, brick, extruded plastic, granite, polystyrene, anthracite, polyester fibres, Lincoln Continentals, lead, manganese, duck, Hawaii... and anything else he can get his teeth on.

About the script

The authors of THE TIME BANDITS have done everything to ensure that this script reaches you as fresh as the day it left the factory. The spelling haz been checked by the Orthers. What you will be reading, and we hope enjoying *(get on with it! – editor)* is a film script. If you are Sean Connery, for instance, you would probably get at least 15 of these to read before breakfast every day *(stop being so creepy to Connery – he's agreed to be in the film, so we can stop all that sort of stuff now – ed.)*, but for those of you who may never have been sent a film script here is some guidance to the technical jargon you will encounter:

Int. "Interior". Every scene has to be labelled "Interior" or "Exterior" so that the crew know whether to bring coats or not.

Ext. "Exterior" *(Latin for "outside" or in England "bloody cold")*

Cut to. Well, I'm sure you know that one.

Pan. Like "dolly," "crab," or "track" it is not, as Eisenstein once jocularly remarked, a cameraman's skin complaint, but a movement of the camera. From side to side or up and down. Film critics can do it without a camera *(keep to the point – ed).*

Out of Shot. Not quite in the picture. A device to save money, as in "Marlon Brando is heard just OUT OF SHOT" or "An Indian uprising begins . . . just OUT OF SHOT." In TIME BANDITS it's used to avoid paying an entire orchestra (on the Titanic, an orchestra plays "OUT OF SHOT").

V.O. Voice Off. Another device for saving money. An actor is here paid for his voice, not his body. In 1953 there was a celebrated version of "Ben Hur" shot entirely in V.O. Two ladies in a South London Launderette sit and overhear the entire story of the slave who rose to the highest position in Rome. It lasted 3¼ hours and cost only £24.00. It's also the only film ever made to take nothing at the box-office. It ran for two weeks at the Odeon Peckham, whilst the cinema was closed for redecoration.

Pull Out. This is what the backers do after they've seen the first rough-cut (Not in the case of the TIME BANDITS though. Here they pulled out even before they saw the rough-cut).
It's also used in the script to denote a camera movement. The camera operator PULLS OUT (i.e. widens focus) from a CLOSE-UP to a WIDE SHOT.

Pull Back. The same sort of camera movement as Pull-Out but we're desperate to fill this book somehow. The Pull-Back or Pull-Out is often used in COMEDY to reveal a joke – as in P.B.T.R.N.T.

P.B.T.R.N.T. Pull Back To Reveal No Trousers. If a joke has not gone particularly well in CLOSE-UP (C.U.) this gives the actor a chance to redeem himself by being revealed to have no trousers on.
You'll be amazed how, even nowadays, there are few audiences who can resist the humour of someone with no trousers on. In fact in 1955, the man who made the Voice-Over (see above) version of "Ben Hur", also re-made Andrej Wajda's "Kanal" trilogy without any trousers on at all. The film was premiered at the Regal, Clapham Common, but the cinema was sadly demolished during the performance.

Fade. An indication to the editor *(of the film, not the book – editor)* that the scene should be gently eased into the scene following, rather than sharply cut (see CUT).

P.O.V. "Point Of View." Strictly a technical term here. It does not refer to any political or moral stance, but simply what the camera sees through the eyes of a certain character. e.g. Kevin's P.O.V. what Kevin is seeing at any particular moment – usually Terry Gillam, face contorted with rage, brandishing an enormous stick. (see "directors").

A.C.T.T. Association of Cinematographic and Television Technicians.

B.M.W. Bayerische Motor Werke.

A.T.I.E.E. Alright. This Is Enough (Editor).

More about the script

In order to give you, the reader, the full flavour of what goes on in a film-script, we have reprinted here almost exactly the script as it was that wonderful April morning when Sean Connery first held it in his firm, tanned hands and *(I told you, we've got Connery, we don't need to do this – editor)* . . . and there are scenes which at a later date received the highest accolade in the screen writers business – to be "deleted". Scenes that were so good, that rather than subject the audience to the ruthless demands of total pleasure and enjoyment, and to avoid moments of hysterical happiness, which can severely damage the fabric of cinema seats, were sadly excised, from the final production. They will join such famous unseen sequences as The Lobster Ballet in "2001", the Highland Games sequence in "Cries and Whispers", the sinking of the submarine in "The Gospel According to St. Matthew" and the open-heart surgery in "Pillow Talk".

A note about "Horseflesh"

Some of you may be concerned about the allusion in the scriptbook to one "Horseflesh", who is neither "OUT OF SHOT" or "V.O." In fact he is N.E. (Non-Existent). The trouble is quite frankly that if HORSEFLESH had been in it he would have made seven dwarves, and we'd have had libel suits from Disney and all sorts of things. But we liked the name, so he remains as the mystery dwarf, and we apologise to Robert Redford whom we might have been about to ask to play the part (crouching of course).

"THE TIME BANDITS"

A Screenplay

by

MICHAEL PALIN

and

TERRY GILLIAM

April 1st 1980

1 SCREEN IN DARKNESS 1

VOICE OVER

It is the beginning of time. The Past has only just begun. Nothing exists save the Supreme Being himself.

And the Supreme Being decreed there should be light.

Light.

.. and with the light there came water and land and fire and ice and volcanoes and thunderstorms and sunshine and wind and suddenly there was work for everybody.

Screen fills with the title ... "THE TIME BANDITS"

By day and by night the servants of the Supreme Being worked away - designing fish and electrifying eels and deciding what colour rainbows should be and whether mountins should slope up or down or camels have feathers, whilst the Supreme Being himself wrestled with the problems of Good and Evil.

1A EXT. HOUSING ESTATE DAY 1A

Mix through from title to a modern housing estate in S.E. England early on a summer's evening. Row upon row of modern houses, all identically sterile, are settled comfortably amongst new trees, grass and neat cul-de-sac roads. The credits roll as we track along. We hear the sounds of various electrical appliances, whizzing and whirring, switches clicking on and off. Hedgecutters, cars being cleaned out by the most modern gadgets. A symphony of semi-urban affluence in 1980. The noises increase gently as we close in on to the upper room of one such house.

CUT INSIDE TO:

2 INT. KEVIN'S BEDROOM DAY 2

In a corner of the room, KEVIN - a rather ordinary but clearly imaginative 11 year old - is busy arranging his toy soldiers and horses into battle formation. Making lots of noise he attacks them with tank and laser gun. Bang! His mounted troops are sent flying. Zap! The building block fortress comes crashing down. Roar! A rocket powered machine spins around the corner and smashes into plastic Indians. He is deeply immersed in this battle as the mismatched forces rage to and fro, when suddenly the mood is broken by his MOTHER's voice from downstairs.

MOTHER (V.O.)
Kevin, supper!

KEVIN pays no attention.

MOTHER (V.O.)
Kevin!

KEVIN
All right!

He looks back at his toys - then, with a quick flick of his foot he does one final apocalyptic wipe-out of troops. Resignedly he heads off out of the room, taking as he goes, a thick book of Greek Heroes. CREDITS END.

3 INT. KITCHEN DAY

KEVIN sits down at table, with his book. His FATHER sits, occasionally slurping a cup of tea and reading the evening paper. There is a ping! from the sideboard and after a moment MOTHER sets a plate of three very similar bland lumps before KEVIN.

KEVIN
(setting aside his book)
What's that ?

MOTHER
(picking up packet from sideboard and studying contents)
"Chicken, duchesse potatoes, and carrots"...

KEVIN looks sceptical.

MOTHER
It says it's lovely.

KEVIN
(unconvinced)
Which is the chicken ?

3 Continued 3

MOTHER
(looks at pack again, rather
irritably this time)
Er... the one on the left ...

KEVIN isolates the chicken and cuts a bit off in a desultory way. He opens the Greek book and reads at the same time.

MOTHER
(addresses FATHER as she throws
pack away)
What we need is something to take these
things out of the packet automatically.
It's wearing me out - all this unwrapping ...

FATHER
We can't have everything dear.

MOTHER
Why ever not ? I know some people who
have.

4 INT. SITTING ROOM EVENING 4

Still picture of modern,fully gadgeted kitchen. Applause. Pull out to reveal it's on a TV screen and Mid-Atlantic voice-over is describing it.

VOICE OVER (on TV)
Yes, folks ... Moderna Designs present
the latest in kitchen luxury. The Moderna
Wonder Major All Automatic Convenience Center-ette.
Gives you all the time in the world to
do the things you really want to do!

CUT TO REVERSE ANGLE. MOTHER & FATHER sit in their armchairs looking zombie-like at the TV screen. They each have a mail order catalogue on their laps. Behind them KEVIN sits immersed in his Greek hero book. He looks up.

KEVIN
Dad ... did you know that ancient Greek
warriors had to learn 44 ways of unarmed
combat ?

The TV drones on.

VOICE ON TV
.. a washing machine that cleans, dries
and tells you the time in three major
international cities! A toaster with a
range of 50 yards! And an infra-red
freezer/oven complex that can make you
a meal from packet to plate in 15½ seconds.

Skippers blast Headingley pitch
Up to Boycott
ATHENS
COACH
The Big Book of Greek Heroes
The Big Book of Greek Heroes

4 Continued 4

MOTHER
The Morrisons have got one that can
do that in 8 seconds.

FATHER
Oh ...

MOTHER
Block of ice to Boeuf Bourgignon in
8 seconds ...
(with feeling)
... lucky things ...

FATHER
Well, at least we've got a two speed
hedge cutter.

KEVIN
Did you know, the ancient Greeks could
kill people 26 different ways!

FATHER
(without turning)
Bedtime for you Kevin, it's nine o'clock.

KEVIN
And this king, Agamemnon, he once fought ..

MOTHER
Go on dear, your father's said!

KEVIN
Oh, all right

4 Continued 4

Meanwhile on the TV screen, a BRUCE FORSYTH figure has bustled on in front of the dream kitchen.

COMPERE
Well, that's today's star prize, so let's meet today's star guests on "Your Money Or Your Life"!

Music.

The title "Your Money Or Your Life" flashes on and off in neon behind him ... as a rather nice OLD COUPLE are brought on by a leggy, fishnet-tighted HOSTESS.

COMPERE
And your names are?

OLD MAN
Mr and Mrs Staveacre.

COMPERE
Oh come on, let's not be so formal ... I'm Ken.

OLD MAN
Yes we know that.

COMPERE
And you are -

OLD MAN
Mr. Staveacre

COMPERE
No, come on! What does you wife call you in those intimate little moments when there's just the two of you? Eh? Alone together Eh..Eh?

OLD MAN
(embarrassed)
She calls me....
(whispers to compere highly confidentially)
Jumbo.

COMPERE
(very loudly)
Jumbo! Well Jumbo it is then..

Roars of laughter from crowd.

COMPERE
And what about you, my dear?

OLD LADY
Beryl.

4 Continued 4

COMPERE
Jumbo and Beryl ... it's Your Money
or Your Life tonight - are you nervous ?

And so on.

5 INT. HALLWAY EVENING

KEVIN pauses on stairs up to bed.

KEVIN
Could we go to Greece one day ?

6 INT. SITTING ROOM EVENING 6

Laughter from TV. CUT TO screen to see that the OLD MAN is blindfolded, and led towards some heavy black weights; 2 floppy ears are put on either side of his head.

COMPERE
Now then Jumbo ... no ... don't lift yet. Oo, you are keen....

FATHER & MOTHER
(without turning)
Good night!

KEVIN turns and walks up to bed. Back to the TV.

COMPERE
Is he like this at home Beryl ? Eager ?

Roars of laughter. BERYL looks embarassed ..

COMPERE
Oo, I bet you have some fun on British Legion night!

More roars of laughter.

And so on!

7 INT. BEDROOM NIGHT

KEVIN is in his pyjamas. Just before he gets in bed he pauses, looks down at his toys, and moves a couple of Napoleonic soldiers into battle position. He then climbs into his bed. He picks up his book and looks at Agamemnon again, with wide eyes.

FATHER (V.O.)
And turn that light off!

KEVIN reluctantly switches off his light. Pauses for a moment. Then snuggles into his blankets and turns over onto his side. The sound of downstairs fades into a strange, deep silence. Suddenly there is the sound of fierce rattling and banging. KEVIN pulls himself up on his elbow. He looks into the darkness anxiously. The weird and violent banging and clanking comes from the wardrobe standing against the wall opposite his bed. Even as KEVIN looks the noise and shaking increase, and suddenly the wardrobe doors burst open - splinters flying everywhere - and a fully-armoured mediaeval KNIGHT on horseback charges out of the wardrobe and into the room. The HORSE is covered in froth, and is rearing wildly.

Continued

YOUR MONEY OR YOUR LIFE

7 Continued 7

almost out of control. A great wind blows through the room swirling leaves and dust about. The KNIGHT has a huge sword in his hand which sweeps through the air knocking objects in the room all over the place. He is shouting after some other knight we can't see. Suddenly, with a commanding cry from the KNIGHT, the HORSE leaps right across the kid's bed and charges down a darkened avenue of trees that has replaced one of the walls of the bedroom. KEVIN is stunned. He dives under the covers. The hoofbeats disappear into the distance and, slowly, he peers out from his hiding place. Everything is back to normal. No mess. No KNIGHT. No avenue of trees. He turns on the light. Getting out of bed he goes over to the wall where the avenue of trees had been. Nothing. Except...among the pictures stuck all over the wall is one which is identical to the avenue of trees down which the KNIGHT vanished. Suddenly, the door of the room is flung open.

FATHER
What the hell is going on up here?
I told you to turn that light off and
get to bed. And <u>no</u> more noise!

7A INT. KITCHEN EVENING 7A

Supper at home. They're all eating identical food. KEVIN is anxious to be somewhere else.

MOTHER
(to FATHER)
It just came off like that ... the
whole thermostat. That's the toaster
the spreader and the slicer all gone.
She's in a <u>terrible</u> state.

FATHER
Should have bought German...

KEVIN
(eagerly)
Mum.... ?

MOTHER
That's just what I said. Would have
matched her rotissomat too....

KEVIN
Mum... Dad... can I -

MOTHER
(turning on him)
And you're going to bed in good time
tonight!

KEVIN
I was thinking I'd go to bed <u>now</u> actually ...

Continued

7A Continued 7A

MOTHER
<u>Now</u>? Certainly not!

FATHER
You must wait until your food's gone down.

KEVIN
I haven't eaten any food...

MOTHER
Well, you <u>must</u> eat your food.

FATHER
Then wait for it to go down.

They are cut short by a new noise. A shrill whining followed by a series of rapid alarm buzzes.

MOTHER
Oh no! Not the carvery again....

She rushes across to a machine that had decided of its own accord to start slicing a joint of cold meat, sending slices of ham quetly and unstoppably on to the floor.

7B INT. SITTING ROOM NIGHT 7B

TV is on again. Same game show - much laughter. This time the OLD MAN is suspended above a large vat of custard. Everyone roars with laughter. Except KEVIN's MOTHER & FATHER.

PULL OUT - KEVIN is in the hall making his way past the sitting room door. He has something hidden under his jumper.

COMPERE
...Ooh you are awful! Now all I want to know is ... what famous film star begins with 'C' ... I'll give you a clue ... it's a lady, a lovely lady who sings and dances...

OLD LADY
C......C......C......

COMPERE
Come on, Beryl, Jumbo's going to end up in the soufflé.....

KEVIN
It's gone down now ... my supper ... I can feel it. I think I'll go to bed.

FATHER
Good, off you go ... but no noise!

7B Continued 7B

A roar of laughter from the TV drowns the end of FATHER's sentence.

KEVIN
What ?

FATHER
No noise!

KEVIN
Oh no! Right ...

OLD LADY whispers something to COMPERE

COMPERE
No no Beryl, Caruso was a man!

KEVIN runs up the last three stairs in a single bound.

THE OLD MAN enters the custard unceremoniously.

7C INT. BEDROOM NIGHT 7C

KEVIN's bedroom. This time there is no dawdling. KEVIN enters briskly, pulls torch and a brand new Polaroid camera carefully out from his sweater, and lays them on his bedside table. He puts his dressing gown on over his clothes and jumps into bed and looks around. Hesitantly he turns out the light.

Blackness. No noise. No rattlings. Nothing odd. He looks disappointed ... silence. PAN ROUND the toys, the cupboard, to KEVIN, who sits on the bed, bolt upright, with his dressing gown on, a satchel slung around him, torch at the ready, Polaroid camera at the ready. Nothing happens. He flashes the torch. Still nothing. He looks around and switches off the torch.

FADE. FADE UP sometime later. KEVIN is having difficulty staying awake, but every time his head drops it jerks him back into wakefulness. He looks across to the door. The light on the landing goes out, and he hears the door of his parents' bedroom shut. He returns to his watching, but his eyes begin to close. He jerks awake then his tired eyes close again. A clock chimes one.

The room is in silence. KEVIN has finally gone to sleep. Suddenly there is a single heavy thud, quite frightening, from the wardrobe. There is a pause. At first KEVIN does not wake, then follows a series of more rapid heavy thuds, followed by muffled cursing and quite undeniably human grunts and groans. KEVIN wakes and cautiously pulls himself up on his elbow. His heart is thumping.

Continued

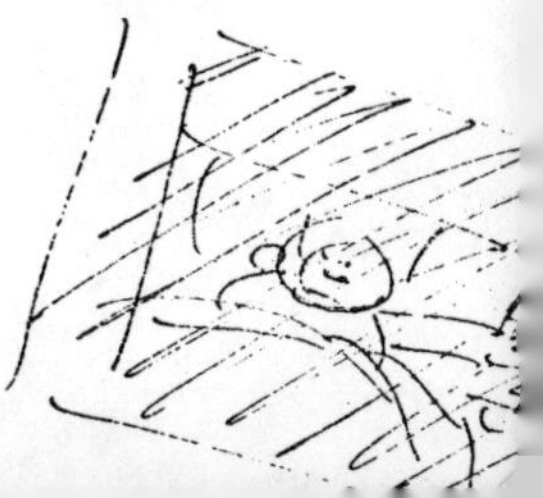

7C Continued 7C

KEVIN can hear his wardrobe door creak open in the dark.

STRUTTER
Where are we ?

RANDALL
I don't know.

WALLY
Look at the map ...

RANDALL
It's not <u>on</u> the map...

WALLY
Is he coming after us ?

RANDALL
Don't panic.

FIDGIT
<u>Is</u> he coming after us?

KEVIN reaches for a torch lying on the bedside table.

RANDALL
I don't know.....I think we gave him the slip.

Hands shaking, KEVIN switches the torch on. Immediately he does so there's panic. The beam of light falls upon a group of DWARVES, dressed and armed in a weird and wonderful variety of costumes and weapons from various periods in history, who blink sightlessly back at him. Their names are RANDALL, STRUTTER, WALLY, OG, FIDGIT and VERMIN.

OG
(fearfully)
It's <u>Him</u> !

They try and race away from the light. Like frightened little animals they rush here and there along the walls.

STRUTTER
(panicked)
He's found us!

WALLY
We're done for!

FIDGIT
I told you...

STRUTTER
We've had it....

7C Continued 7C

They finally pile up in a whimpering heap in the furthest corner.

RANDALL, the apparent leader, hisses to the others.

RANDALL
Leave it to me!

He hesitantly steps forward. He is clutching a parchment map covered in various symbols. He holds it up and addresses the light very deferentially.

RANDALL
...We can explain everything sir..
honestly...we only borrowed the map
sir ... and then we were er ...so happy ...
we just ran off ... in sort ...

7C Continued 7C

RANDALL (Cont)
of high spirits, we were on our way back actually ...
to return the map to you and to ...

KEVIN
Who are you, please ...?

A complete transformation comes over the cowering band.

STRUTTER
That's not Him ...

FIDGIT
Doesn't sound like Him.

WALLY
Doesn't look like Him.

STRUTTER
It isn't Him.

RANDALL
(looking very angry)
Right, come on!

Before KEVIN can hide, the BANDITS as one tear across the room and leap onto the bed. RANDALL jumps across KEVIN's chest issuing orders. KEVIN struggles.

WALLY gets kicked.

WALLY
Ow! My nose!

RANDALL
Help him ... Og, help him!

OG
Who?

RANDALL
Wally One leg each ...

In the struggle, KEVIN and the DWARVES tangled in the bed-clothes topple off the bed. KEVIN's arms are pinioned to the floor.

RANDALL
Strutter ... get his torch ...

STRUTTER grabs the torch.

RANDALL
Right, shine it ... right in the face ...

Continued

Continued

7C

STRUTTER shines the torch full in RANDALL's face.

RANDALL

His face!

STRUTTER shines the torch in KEVIN's face. KEVIN looks terrified.

STRUTTER
It's a kid!

RANDALL
Og...Fidgit ... check the door.

With well-practised precision they run to the door. FIDGIT leaps on OG's shoulders and looks out through the glass light above the door -

FIDGIT
All clear ...!

STRUTTER switches on the small bedside lamp which has toppled to the floor.

RANDALL
(pulling KEVIN to his feet)
Right! You just keep quiet and tell us how to get out of here.

WALLY
He can't.

RANDALL
What ?

WALLY
He can't tell us how to get out of here if he keeps quiet.

RANDALL
(spinning on WALLY)
Shut up!

KEVIN
(still wide-eyed with amazement)
W...W...Why don't you get out the way you came ?

RANDALL
(grabbing KEVIN by the pyjama front pulling himself up to his full height and staring at KEVIN's chest)
Don't try and be smart with me, you little creep ...

Pugnacious murmurs from the other DWARVES as they advance. "Little Clever Dick" - Smartarse!" etc.

7C Continued 7C

RANDALL
If you want to play it smart ... I'll introduce you to Vermin ... he eats anything you know, especially bits of people he doesn't like.
(he indicates leering dwarf at the back)

7C Continued 7C

KEVIN
(beginning to back away)
I'm not trying to be smart ... I'm just trying to help ...

RANDALL
(advancing)
You know ... don't you ...

KEVIN
(backing away)
I don't know anything.

RANDALL
You know - and you're not going to tell us - well I'm getting angry!

KEVIN is pinned back against the wall by this time.

KEVIN
I don't know -

RANDALL
And Vermin's getting hungry ...

KEVIN
Aargh!

The wall he's leaning against suddenly moves back, as RANDALL lunges. KEVIN falls to the floor in amazement.

RANDALL
That's it! He's found it ...

STRUTTER
What ...?

RANDALL
The way out!

KEVIN picks himself up.

KEVIN
It's never done that before ...

RANDALL hands KEVIN the torch.

RANDALL
Hold that ... come on you lot ...
Push!

The excited DWARVES rush to the wall and push. Immediately one lot push with such force the wall moves back several feet, and three others fall on the floor. It's very chaotic. RANDALL tries desperately to organise them.

Continued

7C Continued 7C

RANDALL

Not like that! Wait ...Wait for me
to give the order ... Right ... ready ...

They lean against the wall.

... One! ...

Some of them push, others fall on the floor as the wall moves a few more feet.

RANDALL is beside himself with anger. He stamps his foot vigorously.

RANDALL

Wait! You never start at one!
Whoever heard of anybody starting at
one! ... I'll say "one-two-three" and
on three we heave ...

OG

(who is very, very slow on
the uptake)

We heave on - Two ... or three ?

RANDALL

Three!

At this, the OTHERS push, RANDALL and STRUTTER, who are leaning against the wall arguing, fall to the ground ... The wall is now about ten feet from its original position. RANDALL is about to go mad again when there is a rushing wind ... they all turn ... there behind KEVIN is a bright light ...An ever-widening radiance ... They look in fear.

WALLY

He's found us...!

KEVIN

Who?

RANDALL

(with sudden urgency)

One-two-three ... heave ...!

They all heave ... The wall begins to move steadily but not fast enough.

RANDALL

(to Kevin)

Help us ... help us.... please ..

KEVIN, still wide-eyed with wonder, momentarily stands undecided then, with a look back at the light, begins to push.

RANDALL

That's it. Push! ... Push!

7C Continued 7C

With everyone now pushing out of blind panic, the wall moves back ... 20 ... 30 ... 50 feet. The bedroom assumes the shape of a long corridor with familiar bedroom objects receding into the distance.

The glow increases as the DWARVES scrabble with the wall. It coalesces at last into a brilliant white FIGURE with long beard and leonine head of hair ... the wind howls, swirling his hair and robe about majestically. He heads down the passage at them.

RANDALL
(screams)
Push!

KEVIN
Who is that?

RANDALL
Push!

The DWARVES push frantically. KEVIN looks back in terror and bewilderment. The SUPREME BEING (for it is he) fills the passageway with his awesome presence. He makes to speak. The DWARVES push. The SUPREME BEING levels his gaze upon them and shouts with the authority of many centuries.

SUPREME BEING
Return what you have stolen from me!
Return! Return! ... return the map
or it will bring you great danger ...
Stop! ... NOW!

The DWARVES push, then suddenly, they lose their balance as the wall drops away into darkness. Unable to slow their momentum, they plummet after it into black space.

8 TIME/SPACE 8

As the square of light from the end of the bedroom disappears far above them, they fall. Down, down through the blackness they tumble. Their figures distort... stretching and twisting and then reforming as they pass through galaxies of black spheres in even blacker space. The fall appears to be endless. KEVIN is terrified.

9 EXT. DESERTED FARMYARD DAY 9

CUT TO a deserted farmyard. The farm buildings are in an advanced state of disrepair. A chicken pecks in the dusty yard. Suddenly the CHICKEN emits a terrified squawk and leaps into the air as a cloud of dust explodes in front of her. The dust clears revealing the piled figures of the DWARVES and KEVIN. A slight pause and then OG, the last as usual, splashes into a nearby watertrough. All the GANG scramble to their feet and race off for the barn. RANDALL grabs KEVIN's arm and drags him along.

10 INT. BARN DAY 10

Scattering a few bedraggled geese,they race into the barn and dive into the straw, wriggling out of sight as fast as possible. RANDALL throws KEVIN to STRUTTER.

KEVIN
What is going -

STRUTTER clamps his hand over the BOY's mouth and drags him out of sight. RANDALL hunches down behind a post near the door. He stares intently back at the spot they landed. He holds his breath. After a few tense moments he lets out a sigh of relief.

RANDALL
Cor ... That was close ... All clear!

Slowly the others peer out from their hiding places. STRUTTER releases his grip on KEVIN. The DWARVES begin climbing out of the straw. Their eyes are wide with a mixture of fear and relief.

KEVIN
Who are you?

RANDALL
(rather impatient at the interruption)
... Ssh!

KEVIN
(his voice edged with panic)
Well ... where are we ... what happened to my room ...? Who was that man?

FIDGIT
(the nice one-- next to Kevin)
That was no man ... that was the Supreme Being.

KEVIN
You mean God?

FIDGIT
We never got to know him that well. We only worked for hi ...

RANDALL
(very much playing the leader in the emergency)
Shut up!! Are we all here ...?
(he looks round at the panting bunch of disreputables)
... Wally ...?

WALLY
Sir ...

10 Continued 10

RANDALL
Strutter...?

STRUTTER
Yeah...

RANDALL
Fidgit...?

FIDGIT
Yeah...

RANDALL
Og...?

OG
(doesn't understand the question. He blinks, something he's just learnt)

RANDALL
Are you <u>here</u>?

OG
Mm?

FIDGIT
(helpfully)
Yes he's here ...

RANDALL
Vermin ...?
(he looks around)
... Vermin!

There is a grunt from an ill-lit corner of the bales. It's VERMIN, he quickly secretes some object behind his back, but a few feathers around his mouth give him away. He smiles rather pathetically.

RANDALL
<u>Stop</u> eating!

WALLY
I'd rather he ate them than us ...

RANDALL
Right it's not safe to stay here, he's still after us, so we've got to keep moving ...Og, Vermin .... hey! Where are you going?

KEVIN has made a break for it. He runs out of the barn.

11 EXT. DESERTED FARMYARD DAY 11

KEVIN races out and across the farmyard. He looks left and right, can't see anything.

RANDALL
(from inside the barn)
After him!

12 EXT. COUNTRYSIDE DAY 12

CUT TO KEVIN running down a slope. He jumps a stream ... He looks back and sees the DWARVES at the top of the hill. He races on through a wood, pushes through some undergrowth and onto a dirt road.

13 EXT. ROAD DAY 13

KEVIN
(scrambling out of the undergrowth and onto the road)
Help! Help! Help!

Suddenly, taking in his surroundings, KEVIN stops. He is standing in the middle of an avenue of trees - the avenue of trees down which the KNIGHT from his wardrobe disappeared. His shocked amazement is interrupted by the sounds of thundering hoofbeats behind him. Spinning around, he is practically trampled underfoot by three madly galloping horses ridden by Napoleonic Hussars. The horses rear out of control to avoid the boy. KEVIN stands mesmerized.

1ST HUSSAR
(trying to control his rearing mount)
Dammit boy - these horses are valuable!

2ND HUSSAR
(drawing his sabre and coming at KEVIN)
You little fool!

KEVIN is mesmerized by these live representatives of his favourite toys.

3RD HUSSAR
Leave him, we're late.

He wheels his horse round, the first follows with a kick to his horse's flanks, and heads off. KEVIN, fearless because of his amazement, stands with a sabre only inches from his throat.

2ND HUSSAR
(angrily)
Simpleton!

The 2ND HUSSAR whirls his horse away and charges after the others. The DWARVES who have been watching all this from the cover of the undergrowth, slip off in the opposite direction.

KEVIN turns to where the DWARVES were, but can see no sign of them.

13A EXT. HILL DAY 13A

Wide-eyed, KEVIN rushes up the hill after the HUSSARS. On reaching the brow of the hill he stops - his eyes can't believe what they are seeing. Spread out in front of him is a sweeping panorama of a late 18th century battlefield. In the distance, surrounded by fiercely fighting troops, is a town under heavy bombardment. REFUGEES stream out of the town and up the road towards KEVIN, who is soon caught up in the swirl of the retreat. Trying to get a view of the battle, KEVIN kneels down, peering through the passing cartwheels. One of the REFUGEES stumbles over him.

13A Continued 13A

REFUGEE
(roughly lifting KEVIN up)
On your feet boy ...

MONK DRIVING CARTLOAD OF NUNS
Get a move on! They're taking prisoners ..

KEVIN
Excuse me, what is this town ?

REFUGEE
Castiglione ...
(bitterly)
... or what Napoleon's left of it ...

KEVIN
Napoleon ?

KEVIN stops in his tracks.

REFUGEE
Yes, it's his city now.
(spits)
(to KEVIN)
C'mon boy ... you come with us if you know what's good for you.

KEVIN
(he can't believe any of this)
No thanks ... Napoleon ?!!

KEVIN is caught in the jostling queue of REFUGEES.

PUSHY CHEESE-CARRYING REFUGEE
You're going the wrong way !

14 EXT. BRIDGE DAY 14

CUT TO beneath a bridge. There, hiding beneath the rumbling refugee carts, beside a river, is the GANG, listening to RANDALL who has the map open on his knee.

RANDALL
Now we obviously went a little wrong when we ended up in the brat's bedroom, but don't worry, I'll get you out of this ..

STRUTTER
It's upside down ...

RANDALL
Listen, do you want to run this gang ?

STRUTTER
No ... no ... we agreed ... no leader ...

RANDALL
Right! So shut up and do as I say.

Suddenly there is a shout from above.

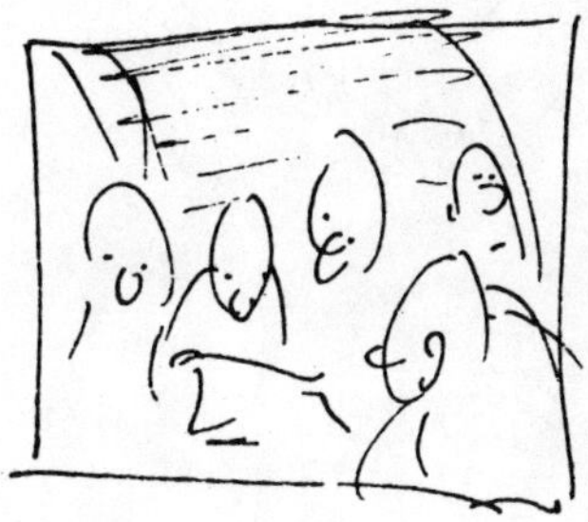

KEVIN
Hey!

They all look up in alarm.

RANDALL
Ssh!

KEVIN comes scrambling down shouting.

KEVIN
(full of eagerness)
Do you know where we are ?

RANDALL
(grabbing him)
Shut up!

KEVIN
(bubbling over)
We're in Italy! ...

RANDALL pushes him down under the bridge.

RANDALL
What the hell do you think you're doing ... yelling and screaming like that ?
(he jabs a finger skywards)
You know what'll happen if the Supreme Being finds us ..
(KEVIN looks deflated)
He can turn us all into used handkerchiefs just like that ...

KEVIN
I'm sorry ... but ... I mean...
it's 1796 ... that's Castiglione ..
(he points towards the
city in amazement)
those are Napoleon's troops ...

They look at each other.

14 Continued 14

RANDALL
Right... So we've got to get into
the town...

KEVIN
Oh... great!

RANDALL
Ssh! Now.....

He is interrupted by a great commotion on the bridge above them. One of the refugee carts that have been rumbling over the bridge stops, and an elderly expiring MAN is being carried down to the water by his two DAUGHTERS or SONS. He's moaning wretchedly....

RANDALL
(shouting up in irritation)
Dammit, can't you flee more
quietly .... I'm trying to concentrate...
Now...

STRUTTER, who had stuck his head out and seen the untended cart, pops his head back in again.

STRUTTER
I've got an idea ... Quick....

All the DWARVES huddle together, then heads nod. Then STRUTTER takes a quick look up at the cart, across to the expiring old MAN. Then gives a signal.

With lightning precision the GANG rush up on to the bridge, surround the cart and throw out all the contents. Then, with clubs, swiftly knock the wheels off. They throw the wheel-less cart over the side of the bridge and it lands in the water. Grabbing a couple of utensils to use as paddles they rush back down to the stream and leap into the floating cart. The last DWARF hands a cup to the old REFUGEE to aid his drinking.

REFUGEE
Thank you kind - here!

He realises with indignation that he's been given his own cup. As the cart floats off down the river the REFUGEES profusely start to thank the DWARF when they realize what has happened. The cartload of fiercely paddling DWARVES floats away toward the setting sun ... and adventure.

15 EXT. CASTIGLIONE NIGHT 15

Cart-boat makes its way through the burning devastation surrounding the stream. BODIES plummet from bridges, TROOPS march to and from. PEOPLE rush to water to escape the flames. Dead ANIMALS float in the stream. Manoeuvring their craft to a landing, the GANG climb out. Over all the horror is the sound of one man laughing.

16 EXT. CITY STREETS NIGHT 16

Entering the ruined city, they make their way past debris and burning buildings. WOUNDED lie about the streets waiting for attention. The BOY and the DWARVES head in the direction of the laughter.

KEVIN 17
(to STRUTTER)
What are we going to do?

STRUTTER
(sharply)
Sssh....

FIDGIT
(whispers)
A robbery...

KEVIN
A robbery?

FIDGIT
(a little indignantly)
Of course... we're international criminals ... we do robberies...

RANDALL
Shh... quiet at the back...

17 EXT. TOWN SQUARE NIGHT 17

In the middle of the demolished town square stands a small open-air theatre surrounded by a low enclosure. On the stage is an even smaller puppet theatre. A loud and violent Punch and Judy show is being performed. Around the edge of the audience area stand impatient and exasperated FRENCH GENERALS. Alone, in the middle of the audience area, sits a small uniformed MAN enjoying himself immensely. It is

17 Continued 17

NAPOLEON BONAPARTE. His laughter carries over the devastation. The town ELDERS are next to the FRENCH GENERALS - in chains. Troops continue to round up townspeople and march them to a wall where they are executed by a firing squad. This continues throughout the entire scene.

Everyone, apart from NAPOLEON, is looking anxiously and nervously at each other ... smoke drifts across the area and there is the sound of distant gunfire.

RANDALL
(to the group, crouched behind a pillar)
That's him ...
(he points to NAPOLEON)

KEVIN
(his face changes)
You're not going to rob <u>him</u> ?

RANDALL
That's right .. every single penny he's got.

KEVIN
That's <u>Napoleon</u> ...

17 Continued 17

RANDALL
And he's rich...

KEVIN
But -

RANDALL
Ssh!

He pushes them back in the shadows, as one of Napoleon's Generals, LUCIEN, passes close by them, and goes across to NAPOLEON. LUCIEN, like all Napoleon's advisers, is unfortunately very tall.

LUCIEN
(leaning down to NAPOLEON)
Monsieur Commander ... I think that the Mayor of Castiglione and his Council would like very much to surrender now please ...

NAPOLEON does not respond. He just roars with laughter at the puppet show.

NAPOLEON
Look at that! Look at the little fellow!
(he convulses with laughter)

LUCIEN
(with a glance towards the other Generals who motion him to have another go)
Sir ... The surrender of Castiglione would be a marvellous feather up the cap ... with this city we have the whole area of Western Lombardy at our feet...

NAPOLEON
Oh, go away -
(he turns back to the stage)
More! More!

INT. BACKSTAGE NIGHT 18

CUT TO the stage. The PUPPETEER is really rather badly wounded but manfully carrying on hitting JUDY with PUNCH despite his bloody wounds, because NAPOLEON is enjoying it all so much. Behind the PUPPETEER at back of stage a very

18 Continued 18

nervous greasy-haired MANAGER is biting his nails. Standing around are various other ACTS who look very miserable. They are all very tall. Out in the square NAPOLEON continues to enjoy himself ...

19 EXT. TOWN SQUARE NIGHT 19

He roars with laughter and applauds. LUCIEN looks desperate, another General, NEGUY, walks briskly across, determined to sort this whole thing out once and for all.

NEGUY
Mon Commander, they are very keen to surrender. They 'ave been here 8 hours -

NAPOLEON
Don't stand so close to me Néguy! I've told you about that before. You on one side ... 'im on the other. It's like being at the bottom of a well.

They retreat a few steps back.

Just because you think I'm small ...

NEGUY
(wearily)
No you're not small ... Commander ... you're not small at all.

LUCIEN
No, not by any means. 5 foot 1 is not small.

NAPOLEON
5 foot 1 and Conqueror of Italy ... not bad eh?

GENERALS
No ... very good indeed.

NAPOLEON returns to the puppets as the curtain draws.

19 Continued 19

NAPOLEON
More! More!

20 INT. BACK STAGE NIGHT 20

Behind stage the wretched PUPPETEER, badly wounded and trying to staunch the flow of blood, hears these shouts of appreciation with utter horror ... He's desperately trying to prepare his puppets for another show despite his precarious grip on life. He looks imploringly at the MANAGER, who himself looks only seconds from his 19th nervous breakdown.

21 EXT. TOWN SQUARE NIGHT 21

NAPOLEON
(still applauding vigorously, shouts to his Generals)
When was the last time a man of 5 foot 1 took Milan ... Huh?

GENERALS
(dutifully)
Oh ... long ago sir ...

The MANAGER appears ... He is frightfully ingratiating.

ITALIAN MANAGER
Ah ... er ... sir ... I ... er ... Thank you ... Thank you very much ... I wonder if you would like to see any of our ... other ... items ... We have Zuzu and Benny ...
(he quickly motions them to come out)
... Fun on a unicycle.

They are both tall and gormless, with only three stilts between them. NAPOLEON waves them away.

ITALIAN MANAGER
No ...? Er ... How about the Great Rumbozo ... he sing and lift heavy things ...

He appears, again far too big.

No ... er ... how about ... ah! This I think you like ... very funny ... the Three Idiots ...

21 Continued 21

He summons them.

ITALIAN MANAGER
...er.. from Latvia ... very funny act. They swallow brushes...

Three very frightened MEN in drag appear .... They are all well over 6 foot.

NAPOLEON
(angrily)
No! No ... they're all freaks ... no-one under 5 foot 6! What kind of theatre are you running?

MANAGER
I'm sorry sir but...
(he is cut off by a volley from the firing squad)

NAPOLEON
More of the funny show ... with the little puppets ... hitting each other... that's what I like ... little things ... hitting each other.

NAPOLEON looks so angry that the MANAGER licks his lips and dares say no more. He pushes his act back.

22 INT. BACK STAGE NIGHT 22

Behind the stage, the PUPPETEER is in an even worse state. He holds PUNCH up ...

23 NAPOLEON cheers. PUNCH falls leaving a trail of blood. NAPOLEON boos. The Punch and Judy booth sways and topples 90 degrees onto its back. The PUPETEER is now an EX-PUPPETEER.

RANDALL
(to STRUTTER)
C'mon!

They run towards the back of the stage.

24 INT. BACK STAGE NIGHT 24

The ITALIAN MANAGER has a gun at his head, when they appear. Brief chat, the ITALIAN MANAGER nods his head.

25 EXT. TOWN SQUARE NIGHT 25

Outside NAPOLEON is looking very fed up, at the demise of the puppets. A THIRD GENERAL, 6 foot 9 inch LOUIS MAROIS, COMTE DE BOSANQUET and EARL OF ORLEANS, approaches NAPOLEON. Luckily for him, just as he is about to speak, there is a tatty fanfare and suddenly the DWARVES tumble onto the stage, remove the puppet show and PUPPETEER and go into a dreadful act. It's brief, and at the end RANDALL signals to a MUSICIAN who plays a chord, and the curtains close. NAPOLEON sits very straight-faced.

26 INT. BACK STAGE NIGHT 26

RANDALL
(to the Manager as they come off stage)
Well?

It's been so bad that the ITALIAN MANAGER wearily loops the curtain rope around his neck and prepares to hang himself when suddenly he hears enormous applause from NAPOLEON. He reacts in amazement. Wasn't this one of the worst acts ever witnessed ? But no! NAPOLEON actually appears on stage, shaking hands with these DWARVES, beaming and happy ... He comes up to KEVIN, and KEVIN almost faints when the great man speaks to him ...

NAPOLEON
(shaking hands with Kevin)
You stick with these boys ... young man ... You have a great future.
(he turns to the Dwarves)
You know you are the best thing that has happened to me since the whole campaign ... I came to conquer Italy because I thought they were all small you know - I heard they was really tiny guys but -

NEGUY and LUCIEN come up on stage.

NEGUY
Sir ... I really think there are more important things -

NAPOLEON
(his patience snapping)
Shut up! Don't you dare tell me my business ... You're dimissed you hear ...! You, Lucien, and all the rest of you. Great streaks of misery.

26 Continued 26

NEGUY 26

But sir...

NAPOLEON

No! From today I have new Generals!

He beams at the DWARVES.

27 INT. BANQUET HALL NIGHT 27

The GANG, dressed in huge French General uniforms, sit around a great dining table heaped high with food. The room is full of the spoils of war, glittering goodies off which the GANG can hardly keep their eyes. NAPOLEON is at the head of the table. He is well into a bottle of cognac, and rambles on the while, to the polite but rather embarrassed BANDITS.

NAPOLEON

Alezander the Great ... Five foot
exactly. Isn't that incredible ...?
Alexander the Great, whose Empire
stretched from India to Hungary ...
One inch shorter than me ....!
Oliver Cromwell ... the only man with
any guts in British history ... not
a big man ... not a big man at all...

CUT to the DWARVES nodding dutifully.

28 EXT. TOWN SQUARE NIGHT 28

Cut to out in the square. There is a slight wind whipping around the pathetic group of town COUNCILLORS waiting to surrender. Beside them huddled round a fire are LUCIEN, NEGUY and the other GENERAL in their underwear - though they still have their swords dangling round their long johns. They look up at the lighted window hopefully.

29 INT. BANQUET HALL NIGHT 29

CUT back to the room

NAPOLEON

Louis XIV... 5 foot 3 ... Henry of
Navarre ... called Henry the Great
... 5 foot 2½ ... Charlemagne ...
a dumpy little 5 footer ...
squat little chap

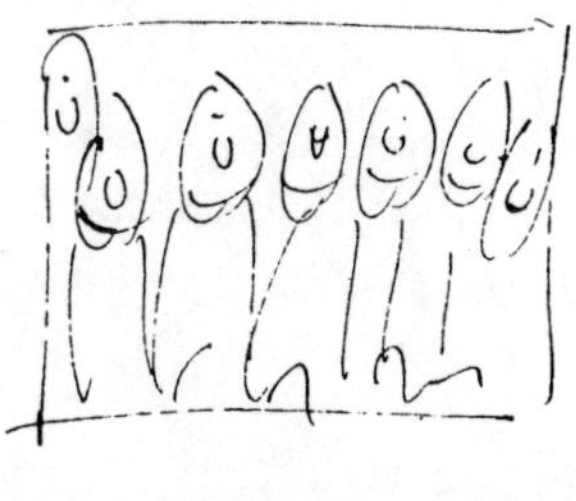

29 **Continued** 29

NAPOLEON is getting more slurred, RANDALL surreptitously opens the map on his knee below the table. He whispers to STRUTTER. We hear NAPOLEON droning on in the background ever more slowly.

NAPOLEON
Charles Martel, 5 foot 3 ...
Saladin ... 5 foot 1, same as me ...
Attila the Hun, 5 foot 1½ ...

RANDALL points out of window, STRUTTER nods.
NAPOLEON is very drunk now. Wind problems rack his body ...
CUT to KEVIN, wide-eyed, but a little saddened, PAN round faces of DWARVES.

NAPOLEON
Voltaire ... 5 ... 2 ... Cyrano de
Bergerac ... 5 ... 3½ ... Tamburlaine
the Great ... 4 foot 9! ... and three
... quarters ...

As we come on to RANDALL, there is a thud, RANDALL looks up. NAPOLEON has finally hit the table and passed out.

OG
(with genuine admiration)
Wasn't he <u>interesting</u> ...

KEVIN looks rather sad, WALLY makes a grab for the brandy. RANDALL smacks his hand sharply.

RANDALL
There's no time for that ... I've
checked the map ... there should
be a time-hole outside ... you go
and find it Strutter....

STRUTTER
Right.

RANDALL
(checking with map
again)
Now ... the hole's here till 12.00
o'clock only ... after that
we're trapped ... so move it!

STRUTTER disappears through the door.

RANDALL
Vermin, Fidgit ... the tapestry ...

29 Continued

FIDGIT
(turns to look at it)
Yes... it's superb isn't it ...
Early 16th century?

RANDALL
Get it.

FIDGIT
Oh...

The BANDITS spring into action ... FIDGIT leaps on VERMIN's shoulders, OG on FIDGIT's and pulls down the tapestry. They start to load the spoils into it.

30 EXT. TOWN SQUARE NIGHT 30

CUT TO the square. STRUTTER, in his ridiculously ill-fitting uniform with long drooping tails emerges from a doorway. GUARD shouts "Attention!" All the SOLDIERS in the area snap to attention - including the reluctant undressed GENERALS. Making his way across the square with as much dignity as possible STRUTTER reaches the spot where the hole should be. He checks the town hall clock. Taking an unexploded cannon-ball he rolls it toward the hole. It disappears.

He smiles with satisfaction and looks up.

CUT to the town hall clock. A minute to midnight. He starts to walk back across the moonlit square with as much speed, and dignity, as he can muster.

31 INT. BENQUET HALL NIGHT 31

Back in the banqueting room. The walls have been stripped back and all the treasure gathered into the tapestry. OG goes across to the sleeping NAPOLEON, takes the rings off one hand, then reaches for the.other hand which NAPOLEON had tucked into his tunic, and removes it. It turns out to be gold and very precious. They unscrew NAPOLEON's hand and drop it in the swag bag.

STRUTTER enters in agitation.

STRUTTER
Thirty seconds!

This galvanises everybody.

31 Continued 31

RANDALL
Let's go...

OG and VERMIN and FIDGIT pull the swag.

RANDALL
(to KEVIN)
C'mon .. don't just stand there.

They start to heave it out. KEVIN takes one last regretful look at his pissed hero.

31A INT. STAIRCASE NIGHT 31A

The GANG drag their swag down the stairs.

32 EXT. TOWN SQUARE NIGHT 32

The GUARDS shout attention as Strutter appears at the doorway. All the SOLDIERY stiffens to attention.

STRUTTER
About turn!

All the SOLDIERS turn away. From the doorway comes the GANG dragging their swag. They make their way through the ranks of SOLDIERS' backs. One of the undressed GENERALS gets suspicious and sneaks a backwards glance. He begins to shout orders to the TROOPS when he sees what's happening. The GANG breaks into a run. SOLDIERS make chase. The town hall clock reads only seconds from the deadline. The GANG madly races for the hole and, just as the clock strikes, disappears. Pursuing SOLDIERS leap for the spot but, nothing happens. The GENERALS in underwear madly shout orders but the GANG and the goodies are gone. Pursuing SOLDIERS leap onto a growing pile of bodies where the hole was.

33 TIME/SPACE 33

The GANG and their bag of swag tumble through blackness, distorting, twisting, reforming as they fall.

34 EXT. FOREST ROAD DAY 34

CUT TO a coach and pair flying through a forest. The style is mediaeval. Inside this hurrying conveyance, sit a well-dressed YOUNG MAN and a breathless YOUNG WOMAN. They are frightfully British. He is called VINCENT, she is called PANSY. Luckily for both of them.

35 INT COACH 35

PANSY
Sir Vincent, you came for me!

VINCENT
Good Mistress Pansy, I could not have ridden faster; 4 horses have I exhausted this day from Nottingham.

PANSY
The way you leapt up to my chamber; so full of manliness.

VINCENT
I could scarce restrain the rushing of my feet. These 12 long years have been like chains that bound me.

PANSY
And the personal problems?

VINCENT
Much, much better. Now my dearest we shall ride full tilt to Dover and there embark for France.

PANSY
You don't have to wear the special -

VINCENT
No, I don't have to wear anything special ... Now Pansy my love.

PANSY
How about diet?

VINCENT
Well, I'm supposed to avoid milk and eggs ... but you are my milk and eggs, Pansy darling.

PANSY
And cheese?

VINCENT (playfully)
Yes ... you're my cheese ... my little cheesy cheese.

PANSY (rather sharply)
No ... d'you have to avoid eating cheese?

VINCENT (getting a little irritated)
Yes ... No ... I don't know ... What does it matter now that we're together ...?

PANSY
My father said it might be catching ...

35 Continued 35

VINCENT
Of course it's not catching .. it was all in the mind anyway ... It only happened when I got worried or over anxious.

PANSY (reassured at last)
Well, you need have no worries now Sir Vincent....

VINCENT
No... no more worries now...

As their lips move remorselessly towards each other there is a sudden rending crash and 6 BANDITS, KEVIN, and a jangling bag full of Napoleonic swag come crashing through the roof of the conveyance.

VINCENT
Aargggghhhh!

PANSY screams.

VINCENT
Bandits! Oh my God.

WALLY
We've landed.

They flail about in the coach - arms and legs, gold objects everywhere...

PANSY
Don't become over-anxious sweetheart...

VINCENT (hysterically)
I'm <u>not</u>!

With a ripping of fabric the DWARVES and their booty fall through the back of the vehicle.

36 EXT. FOREST ROAD DAY 36

The GANG, swag and all, fly out of the now madly swerving coach, and tumble in a heap onto the floor of the forest glade. There they lie surrounded by gold trinkets and amongst them Renaissance masterpieces.

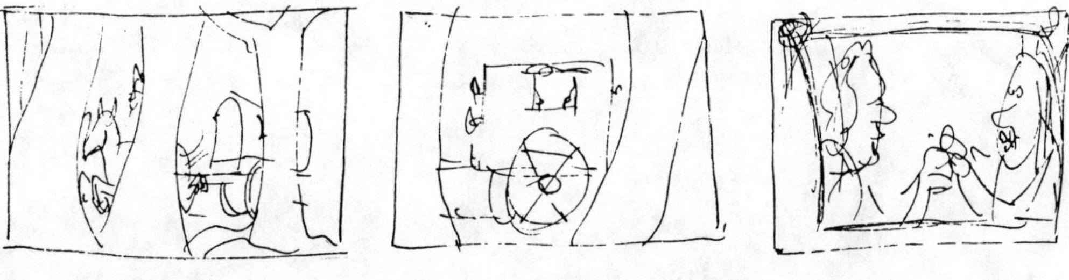

36 Continued 36

WALLY (looking around as if he can hardly believe it)

We did it ...

FIDGIT (Slowly picking himself up)

We did it!

In the distance the coach swings, swerves wildly, does a figure of eight and crashes spectacularly. PANSY's voice rises helpfully from inside the wreckage.

PANSY

Don't worry about a thing darling.

STRUTTER

We did it!

RANDALL

Of course we did it! I tell you stick with me you can't go wrong.

WALLY

Sometimes I almost believe you Randall ...

RANDALL throws a priceless ornament at WALLY it misses and hits OG. OG smiles.

In the distance a hysterical VINCENT who's totally lost his bottle is scrambling out of the coach.

VINCENT

Get the money ... quick! Quick!

PANSY

Your problem, dearest.

VINCENT

Forget the problem ... get the money!

They rush off, casting a last look at the GANG, who are all picking themselves up now and have no intention of chasing them.

FIDGIT

Where are we?

36 Continued 36

RANDALL
Well ... we're obviously ...
(he turns the map around and studies it authoritatively .. he's bluffing)
... er ...

KEVIN
(in wonderment to himself, looking towards the wrecked coach)
... in the Middle Ages ...

RANDALL
(quickly)
... in the Middle Ages ...

Expressions of amazement from the GANG.

RANDALL
(confidently now)
... 500 years before the man we just robbed is even born ...

A pop as a cork comes off a Napoleonic bottle. Cheers from the elated GANG.

Various shouts ... "How about that!" "Try that in a court of law!" ... cavorting and whooping....

VERMIN is eating a porcelain figure of the goddess Ceres.

WALLY
That's not meant to be eaten!

VERMIN
You never know till you've eaten it.

KEVIN (looking around at the almost
(hysterical jubilation)
Are you always like this when you've done a raid ?

FIDGIT
We've never done one before!

36 Continued 36

There's a bit of silence throughout the group at this, apart from VERMIN, who is biting into a clock. They look at each other, and at FIDGIT - should he have told a rank outsider this ?

KEVIN
I thought you were international criminals ..

A pause.

RANDALL
Going to be ... going to be!

This breaks the tension and everyone eases up.

FIDGIT
Yes that's right ... going to be ... specially now we've got Kevin ...

RANDALL
Hang on! Hang on! He's a kid ... he's not one of us.

FIDGIT
He knows an awful lot, Randall.

WALLY
And he's bigger than any of us.

STRUTTER
We always need another pair of hands Randall ... especially with Horseflesh gone ...

They all pause ... something painful has just been mentioned.

KEVIN
Horseflesh ?

36 Continued 36

STRUTTER
(sadly)
He used to work with us ...

WALLY
(emotionally)
One of the best.

ALL
(nodding thoughtfully)
Yeh, yeh ...

VERMIN
(who has been preoccupied with
the while with his own eternal
quest for food, breaks the mood with
a shout of delight)
Hey! Look at this!
(he's opened a big hamper)
Napoleon's packed lunch!

They all happily descend on the contents - chicken legs, pies, cakes, etc. etc. RANDALL stays outside this hysteria. As KEVIN makes to grab some food, RANDALL takes him on one side.

RANDALL
You want to join us ?

KEVIN
Can we really go anywhere ... at anytime ?

RANDALL
You name it. If it's down here ...
(tapping map impressively)

KEVIN
How ?

RANDALL
Because ... this used to belong to
the Supreme Being ?

KEVIN
You stole it ?

RANDALL
Well sort of ... you see, he was our
employer ...
(disbelief from KEVIN)
We helped to make all this ...
(he indicates woodland - KEVIN
looks round duly impressed)
He'd do the big stuff - good and evil,
night and day, men and women - and we did
the trees....

36 Continued 36

KEVIN
(looking around at the sylvan
glade this idyllic medieval afternoon)
That's not bad ...

RANDALL
Exactly ... but did we get a thimbleful of
credit ?

36 Continued 36

The GANG are busy eating.

RANDALL
Oh no ... all we got was the sack ...
for creating the Pink Bunkadoo.

KEVIN
The Pink Bunkadoo?

RANDALL
Yeah... lovely tree, OG designed it ...
six hundred feet high, bright red ...
and smelt terrible...

VERMIN belches loudly, OG pours wine over his head.

RANDALL
Well, as a disciplinary measure we
were sent down to the Repairs Department.
You see, he'd just created evil and was
having a bit of a problem with it.
The fabric of the Universe was sort of
a botch-up job to be quite frank. You see
Kevin...
(he becomes serious and
confidential)
.... there are holes in it....

KEVIN
Holes?

RANDALL
Yes... holes in Time and Space.

KEVIN
Hey! Brilliant.

RANDALL
That's where this comes in ... it's
the map showing where they are, and
it's the only one in existence.
So why repair the holes?
Why not use them ... to get stinking rich...?

WALLY
Yeah .... here's to being stinking rich!

ALL
Stinking rich!

He raises his bottle. The others echo the toast and hold
out the goblets, or in some cases anything they can find
helmets, shakos, boots, etc.

36 Continued 36

FIDGIT
And here's to Kevin...

STRUTTER
Yeah ... Kevin ...

WALLY
Kevin!

OG (confused)
... Stinking Kevin...

ALL
Kevin.... Kevin...

KEVIN looks round with a flush of excitement, then delves in his bag and produces his Polaroid camera.

KEVIN
Hey! Hold it there! Now... smile!

36 Continued 36

They all stand glasses raised ... RANDALL with the map. Various mutters and jokes from the group.

KEVIN points the camera.

KEVIN
Smile ... !

This instruction has awful and truly grotesque effects. A wondrous selection of charmless leers and grimaces. The photo is just taken when there is a terrified scream from deep in the wood. It's unmistakably PANSY.

PANSY
Help! Robbers!

OG
That's us.....!

PANSY screams again.

RANDALL
Someone's in trouble - come on!

The GANG pick up their swag and run off up the track.

37 EXT. FOREST GLADE DAY 37

CUT TO the DWARVES and KEVIN arriving at a glade just in time to see that VINCENT and PANSY have been lashed to a tree by a group of the most FOUL and REVOLTING ROBBERS you could ever wish not to see. They are stripping our 2 young (ish) lovers of all their wealth and fine clothes.

From behind the cover of trees RANDALL and THE BANDITS look on. In wide-eyed admiration.

STRUTTER
Now those are our sort of people

The FOUL and REVOLTING ROBBERS finish their depredation and with much evil chuckling make off. Spitting and swearing filthily as they go.

WALLY
(admiringly)
Now that's what I call style...

37 Continued

RANDALL
Come on!

The DWARVES emerge from their hiding place as PANSY cries one last desperate "Help!"

37 Continued 37

PANSY
(to VINCENT)
At last! Someone's coming!

The DWARVES rush past them and off in admiring pursuit of the ROBBERS.

PANSY
Help! I say! My fiance
and I would care for some help.

VINCENT
Oh no ... I can feel it ... I can
feel the problem again.

PANSY
Don't worry about anything.

VINCENT
Fruit.... I must have fruit.

PANSY
Hey! I say chaps!

But the DWARVES pass by without a look. There is a thunderclap. It starts to rain on them. Quite heavily.

38 EXT. ANOTHER PART OF THE FOREST DAY 38

CUT TO the GANG wandering in the woods. They've lost the evil gang, and are walking fearfully.

RANDALL
(with sublime confidence)
Come on! Don't be so wet....

RANDALL walks authoritatively off. They haven't gone a pace before they tread all unawares upon carefully laid snares and within an instant they are all whisked up on ropes and left dangling upside down from the branch of a tree. As they swing (somewhat chastened by this turn of events) we see a group of the FOUL and REVOLTING ROBBERS in rough mediaeval garb emerge from the ambush. They approach the dangling DWARVES...

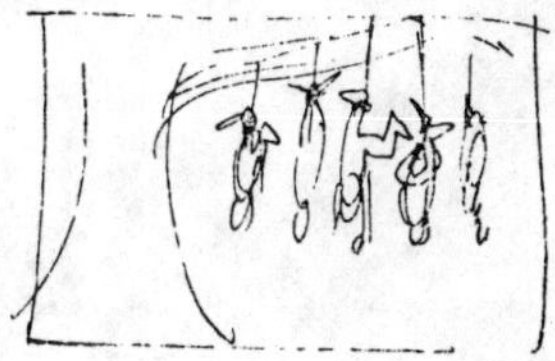

RANDALL
(to WALLY hanging beside him)
Leave this to me, Wally.

WALLY
(suddenly scared stiff)
What do we do?

RANDALL
Just treat them right ... that's all.

RANDALL's upside-down POV of the revolting ROBBER as he approaches.

RANDALL addresses him.

RANDALL
What do you want, you tatty old scumbag?

ROBBER LEADER
(spits out viciously)
Your business ... gobface?

RANDALL
Robbers....

ROBBER LEADER
<u>Villainous</u> robbers.....?

RANDALL
The worst...

ROBBER LEADER
Stop at nothing?

RANDALL
Nothing....

ROBBER LEADER
Steal the cup from the beggar's hands?

RANDALL
Of course....

38 Continued **38**

ROBBER LEADER
Teeth from blind old ladies....?

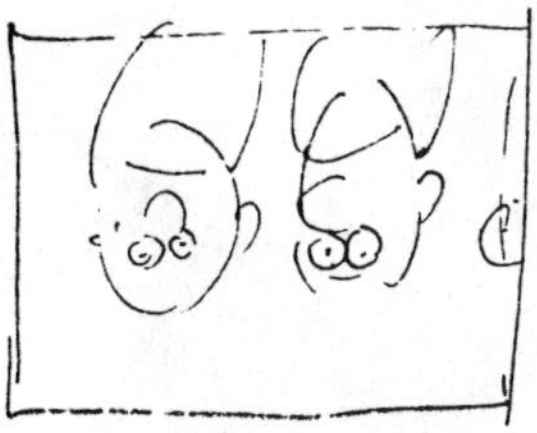

RANDALL
<u>Rather</u>!

ROBBER LEADER
Toys from babies ...

RANDALL
Whenever we can ...

ROBBER LEADER
Right...let them down...they're alright.

The GANG are lowered rather sharply to the ground.

ROBBER LEADER
You looked a horrible lot, but then so does everyone these days.
(he spits revoltingly)

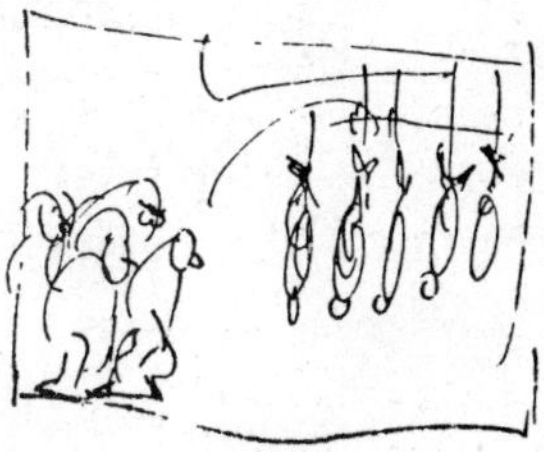

RANDALL
Yeah ... I know what you mean ...
(he feels it's up to him to spit equally revoltingly)
Are you the leader then ?

ROBBER
No ... no ... I'm just a sort of front man .. to give a good impression ... you know.

A light fart from behind one of the evil gang.

RANDALL
(playing it tough)
Well, we only want to talk to the boss, don't we ?

OTHERS
(trying to be nasty)
Oh ... yeah ... yeah ...

ROBBER LEADER
(with a look of fear)
You want to see the <u>boss</u>!

FIDGIT
(quickly)
Well ... not necessarily ...

38 Continued 38

RANDALL
(cutting him off)
Yeah..yeah.. We've got a few ideas for a partnership... a link up... Our gang and his gang, you know.

ROBBER LEADER
Are you serious ?

RANDALL
(carrying on with the bluff, tho' the rest of his gang are looking a little uneasy)
Oh yeah....
(indicates swag)
Wait till he sees what we've got in here.

One of the FOUL and REVOLTING ROBBERS goes for the swag. RANDALL steps in front firmly.

RANDALL
Ah....ah! Only for the boss....

ROBBER LEADER looks round at his hideous gang.

ROBBER LEADER
All right...you asked for it.... follow me .....

As they walk, ROBBER 3 looks at KEVIN, double-takes. Looks again.

ROBBER 3
Hey! This one looks a bit clean.....

FIDGIT (covering as quickly as he can)
No...no....it's a skin complaint.

ROBBER 3
Doesn't look as though that little face has known much evil eh ?

As ROBBER 3 approaches threateningly, RANDALL motions to WALLY and WALLY slips unobtrusively round behind ROBBER 3.

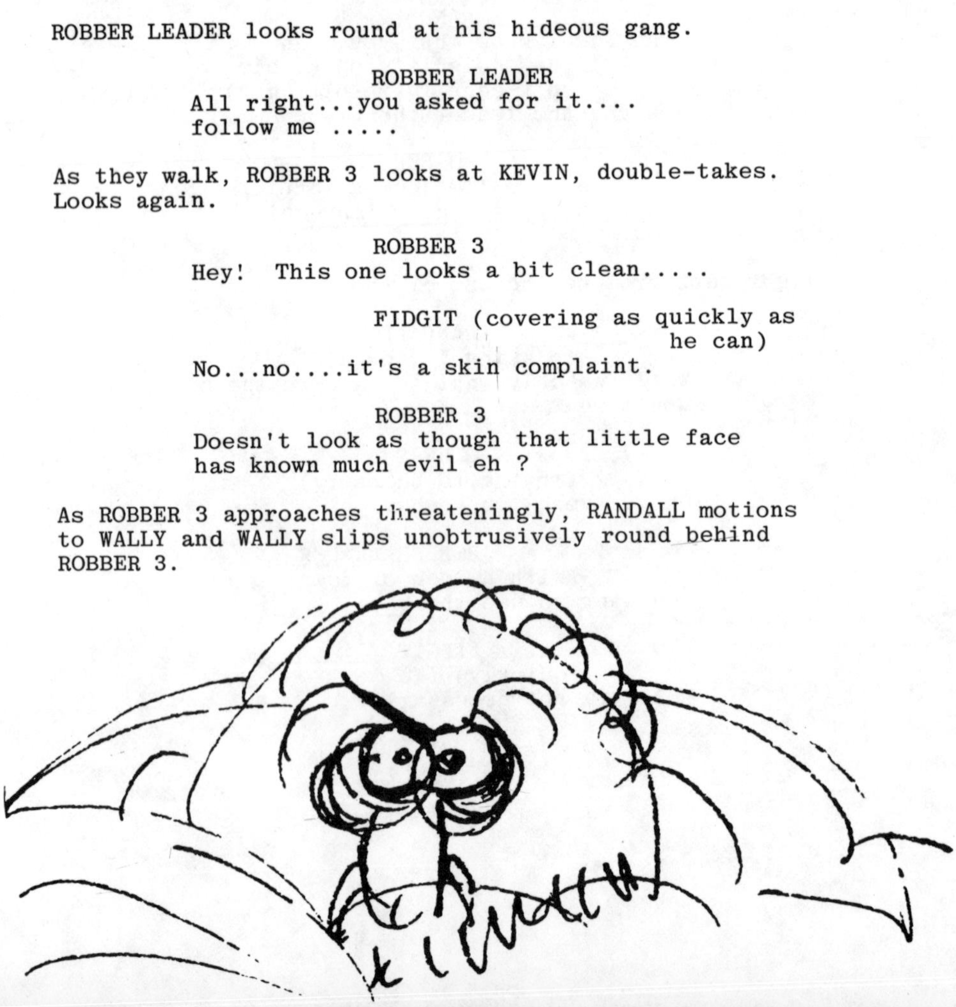

38 Continued 38

KEVIN looks very frightened. The OTHER ROBBERS turn to see what's going on.

ROBBER 3
(who is like all of them, scarred and grubby of countenance)
I think this happy little visage ought to look a little more lived in ... eh boys ...? I mean rogues should look like rogues, I say...

As tension mounts ROBBER 3 reaches for the dagger that hangs in a small sheath at this side. As he does so, WALLY, with well-practised skill, removes the dagger swiftly and quite unnoticeably from the sheath.

ROBBER 3 grabs the dagger but finds himself holding thin air. He turns with a frown to see where it is. WALLY slips deftly to the other side of him and as he"s turned away slips the dagger into KEVIN's hand.

KEVIN
(ingenuously)
Is this yours....?

He holds the dagger out. There is a pause, then everyone roars with laughter ... ROBBER 3 looks very pissed off. He grabs his knife back and takes a swipe at KEVIN.

ROBBER 3
Little thief...!

39 EXT. BANDIT'S HIDEWAY DAY 39

A few rough tents as of a nomadic band. Many more evil looking CHARACTERS are there, fighting and having spitting competitions ... all rather unpleasant. One MAN arm-wrestles ANOTHER and his arm comes off, much laughter. He drops arm onto a pile and shouts:

ARM WRESTLER
Come on you lot ... I like a challenge!

The GANG enters the compound amid shouts of "Who's this?" etc., and are marched up to the main tent...

39 Continued 39

ROBBER LEADER
Wait. I'll tell him you're here ..

He goes into the tent. A pause, then a tall rather well-meaning chap in Lincoln Green appears. KEVIN registers him immediately, his eyes light up and his mouth falls open.

39 Continued 39

ROBIN HOOD
(emerging from tent. He looks and speaks rather like the Duke of Kent)
Hello, I'm Hood.

KEVIN
(nudging FIDGIT)
It's Robin Hood!

ROBBER
(yelling at them)
Say good morning, you scum.

Such is the intimidating force of his yell that they all immediately say

GANG
Good morning, you scum.

ROBIN HOOD
Good morning. You're all robbers, then.

RANDALL
The best, Mr. Hood.

ROBIN HOOD
Jolly good.
(to OG)
And you're a robber are you ?
(no reaction)

Jolly good.
(to WALLY)
And do you enjoy robbing then ?

WALLY
Well it helps pay the rent, sir.

ROBIN HOOD
Ha, ha, ha, ha, ha, jolly good, ha ha.
(to STRUTTER)
And you're a robber too are you ? And how long have you been a robber ?

STRUTTER
Four foot one.

ROBIN HOOD
Good Lord ! Jolly good. Four foot one ?

STRUTTER
Yes.

ROBIN HOOD
Well that is a long time, isn't it ?
Well now, I hear you have made a pretty good haul.

FIDGIT
Well see for yourself sir.

39 Continued 39

The two of them come forward with the haul and lay it down. They drop the edges of the cloth and stand around it. RANDALL eyes ROBIN HOOD with defiant pride.

ROBIN HOOD
Gosh! I say! Crikey! I mean, I've been in robbing for years, and I've never seen anything like this! Crumbs! You acquired all this by yourselves!

RANDALL positively glows. KEVIN looks very chuffed and hopes he will catch his hero's eye.

RANDALL
Well it was a good day, Mr. Hood.

ROBIN HOOD
Jolly good day.

RANDALL
It is nice, isn't it ?

ROBIN HOOD
Rather! I mean what can I say ? Thank you, thank you, thank you all very very much indeed.

RANDALL
Don't mention it - what ?

The grins turn to puzzled frowns from all bar OG, who is still grinning beatifically.

ROBIN HOOD
Well I mean it's frightfully kind of you, the poor are going to be absolutely thrilled. Have you met them at all ?

RANDALL
Who ?

ROBIN HOOD
The poor.

RANDALL
The poor ?

ROBIN HOOD
Oh you must meet them, I just know you'll like them. Charming people, of course they haven't got 2 pennies to rub together but that's because they're poor - ha ha ha.

Laughter all round encouraged by robbers.

ROBIN calls to a dark-browed NEANDERTHAL THUG.

ROBIN HOOD
Marion, would you be so kind as to ask the poor to come in please ?

39 Continued 39

MARION
No problem.

MARION goes off.

ROBIN HOOD
Thank you so much. Yes, well now let's just see what we've got here. This is going to be so much help in our work.

He starts to sort through the treasure ...throwing the objects onto various piles.

RANDALL
No, you don't understand.

ROBIN HOOD
Ah, you mean you need a receipt for tax ?

RANDALL
No, no,all this stuff is ours, we've stolen it.

ROBIN HOOD
Oh yes, I know, and believe you me, the poor are going to be, well not just absolutely thrilled, but also considerably less poor, aren't they Redgrave ?
(picks up gold vase and shows it to Robber Derrick O'Connor)

Gibberish from O'CONNOR.

ROBIN HOOD
You see - what did he say ?

MARION
He said, yes, what with Christmas coming up and all.

MARION starts organising a line of poor PEASANTS who are each given one of the GANG's treasures.

ROBIN HOOD
Ah! Jolly good.
(gives vase to one of POOR)
Well there we are - congratulations - well done.

O'CONNOR belts 1ST POOR MAN in face.

ROBIN HOOD
(hands piece of gold to 2ND POOR MAN)
There you are - well done - congratulations.
(O'CONNOR belts 2ND POOR MAN)
Is that absolutely necessary ?

Gibberish from O'CONNOR.

MARION
He says yes, he's afraid it is.

39 Continued 39

ROBIN HOOD
Ah, fine, fine. There we are madam.
Well done, jolly good.
(O'CONNOR belts POOR WOMAN)
Incidentally, would any of you like to stay
on a bit and help us with our work ? There's
still so much wealth to redistribute.

KEVIN's eyes light up....

KEVIN
Oh, I'd like to stay.

ROBIN turns to him.

ROBIN HOOD
Jolly good ! What's your name ?

This is a great moment for KEVIN. He's just about to say something to his hero, when RANDALL pulls him away.

KEVIN
K...

ROBIN HOOD
K ? What a jolly nice name. Well
never mind - cheerio. Thank you very
much. Thank you very much. Thank you
very very very much.

The DWARVES turn away and with as much dignity as possible, RANDALL leads his MEN off. Some of them cast longing glances back at the rapidly re-distributing wealth.

RANDALL
(between gritted teeth)
If he says thank you once more, I'll
kill him.

ROBIN HOOD
Thank you very very very much.

40 EXT. FOREST GLADE EVENING 40

A fork of lightening cracks across a darkening, wild, forbidding sky. Rain pours down. The atmosphere is suddenly very different. It is dark and dangerous, and a storm is brewing...the GANG are strung out single file. They have to shout to make themselves heard as they straggle back.

As they emerge into a glade there are VINCENT and PANSY, soaked to the skin, still lashed to the tree. A ruthless gang of MONKS - who have taken a strong vow of eternal acquisition - are robbing the couple of their last belongings.

The DWARVES ignore the wretched COUPLE.

RANDALL
We are not a charity organisation..
We're thieves!

KEVIN
We could at least have stayed and talked
to him.

VINCENT
(pathetically)
Excuse me! Excuse me!

40 Continued 40

KEVIN
I'll never get a chance to meet
Robin Hood again.

PANSY
I say! Any possibility of a rescue over here?

All ignore her.

RANDALL
Stop moaning! He's obviously a
dangerous man, unbalanced if you ask me ...
giving away what isn't even his!

KEVIN
That's what Robin Hood always did,
I know that ...

RANDALL
Oh of course you know it all

KEVIN
He's one of my heroes

RANDALL
Heroes!
(he spits)
What good are heroes? What do they
know about a days work - mm?

40 Continued 40

STRUTTER
Leave him alone, Randall ...

40A EXT. ROCKY STREAM EVENING 40A

RANDALL turns on the others. Confrontation in the rain ...

RANDALL
Well, it makes me sick! Anyone who's always right makes me sick.

FIDGIT
That's why you get on with yourself so well ....

RANDALL
Watch it.

STRUTTER
Yeah ... big mouth!

WALLY
Horseflesh wouldn't have got us into this.

RANDALL
Horseflesh is dead.

WALLY
Give me the map. I'm taking over.

RANDALL
Leave it!

STRUTTER
I'm taking over.

FIDGIT
I'm taking over.

A punch up starts here.

Punches are thrown, as they all try to grab the map and they fall into a fight. KEVIN tries unsuccessfully to part them, but they are into a full-blooded punch-up. KEVIN suddenly stops aware that the rain has lessened. He stands aside from the fighting BAND. A cold wind blows suddenly. KEVIN looks a little frightened. The wind increases. The DWARVES fight (slithering around in 2 feet of mud). THE PICTURE WOBBLES.

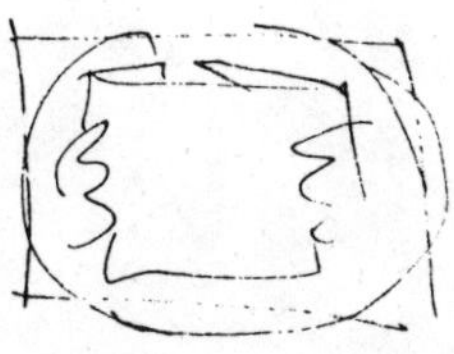

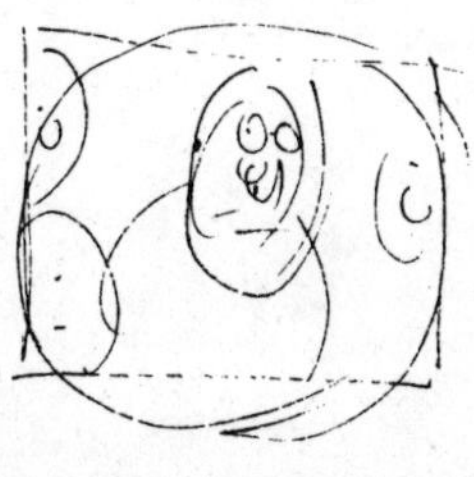

41 INT. EVIL'S GROTTO NIGHT 41

We PULL BACK to reveal that the GANG's image is now seen to be in a watery pool somewhere in a dank, dripping stone chamber. Cabalistic symbols are just visible on the massive stone columns from the shiny floor. In heavy sinister shadows a black shape stands watching. This is EVIL (Arthur G. Evil). Behind him is a cluster of shapes: MR. BAXI-BRAZILIA III, BENSON, ROBERT and CARTWRIGHT, and two SMALL UNIDENTIFIABLE SHAPES. All of EVIL's henchmen are extremely thick.

Evil laughter from them all.

EVIL
So these are the sort of people the Supreme Being allows to steal his map, eh.....?

Laughter from behind.

Look at them... the stunted little proles... I wouldn't trust them to wipe their own noses....

Laughter. Encouraged by the ready sycophantic response, he half turns to a monstrous assistant, BAXI-BRAZILIA III

Eh?

B.B.III
No .. no sire ... much too difficult for them.

EVIL GENIUS
What sort of so-called "Supreme Being" allows silly pratts like that to steal his map? Such a Supreme Being must be a complete and utter idiot, must he not ?

All nod.

B B.III
Well.... he created you, Evil One.

EVIL GENIUS
.... What did you say ?

B.B.III
Well, he can't be a complete idiot, Your Wickedness ... I mean if he created you in all your bad ....

41 Continued 41

EVIL turns sharply. Eyes blaze. He raises a hand. There is a sharp report, a crack and a hiss and the hapless B.B. III ends up in a little smouldering pile.

EVIL
Don't ever say that! No-one created me!
I am Evil, Evil existed long before good.
I made myself and I cannot ever be "unmade"..!
I am all powerful.

Applause.

CARTWRIGHT
(helpfully)
But why, in that case, are you unable to escape from this fortress?

EVIL whips round, raises hand, and zaps CARTWRIGHT horribly. A crack, a hiss and he too is reduced to a smouldering pile. (This is becoming an expensive conversation).

EVIL
Good question. Why do I let the Supreme Being keep me here in the Fortress of Ultimate Darkness ?

ROBERT
(helpfully)
Be.... cause ...

EVIL
Shut up! I am speaking rhetorically.

ROBERT
Of course.

EVIL
I allow him to keep me here in order to lull him into a false sense of security.

ROBERT
...Clever ...

EVIL
But when I get the map, I shall escape from here and then the world will be very different ... because I have understanding.

ROBERT
Understanding of what, oh Nastiness ?

41 Continued 41

EVIL
Of digital watches ... and soon I shall have understanding of video cassette recorders and car telephones, and when I understand them I shall understand computers, and when I understand computers I shall be the Supreme Being.

A SHAPE has scuttled to his side and is pointing excitedly into the pool. The SHAPE is SUGAR RAY BENSON.

BENSON
Sir... Sir...

EVIL
(in full flow now, he doesn't notice)
God is not interested in technology... he knows nothing of the potential of the micro-chip or the silicon revolution. He's obsessed with making the grass grow and getting rainbows right...

BENSON
Sir!

EVIL
(warming to his theme with huge reserves of indignant contempt)
Look what he spends his time on ... 43 species of parrot! Nipples ... for men!

ROBERT
(helpfully)
Slugs....

EVIL
Slugs!
(almost incoherent with contempt.. he laughs a mirthless laugh)
He "created" slugs! They can't speak, they can't hear, they can't operate machinery... I mean are we not in the hands of a lunatic? Mmmmm ?

Much heavy nodding from his intellectually minimal subordinates.

BENSON
Sir... look.....!

EVIL
... I mean ... if I were creating a world ... I wouldn't mess around with butterflies and daffodils ... I would have started with lasers. They would have been 8 o'clock on Day One!

41 Continued 41

With a dramatic flourish, he spreads his arms high and a beam zaps unintentionally from his fingers into the darkness behind him. A brief agonised cry. EVIL turns ...

EVIL
... Sorry!

ROBERT
I can't wait for the new technological dawn.

BENSON tugs at EVIL's sleeve. Irritably EVIL turns.

EVIL
What is it, Benson ?

BENSON
(beside himself with excitement at the news he has to impart)
The map sir ... the map! They've got it with them!

EVIL
What!

BENSON
(jabbing excitedly at the pool)
I saw the map, Awful One ... just now!

EVIL
Are you sure ?

EVIL crosses to the pool.

BENSON
Yes, I'm sure, Master ... down there ... I saw it ... the little one has it.

EVIL (looking at the DWARVES)
The little one ?

BENSON
This is our chance. This is what we've been waiting for.

EVIL peers into the pool. His minions also look in excitedly.

ROBERT
It will set us free.

Minions grunt with excited agreement.

41 Continued 41

EVIL
Shut up! If you are wrong, Benson, my revenge will be slow and unpleasant. I will turn you inside out over a very long period ....

BENSON
Oh thank you, Master, thank you.

EVIL
Now we must bait the hook, see if they bite, and then pull them in.

ROBERT and BENSON react with enthusiasm but are mystified by this use of the metaphor, pedestrian though it is.

EVIL
(to his assembled minions)
Stand by for Mind Control ...

EVIL folds his arms with an impressive flourish, and accidentally zaps himself.

EVIL
Ow!

42 EXT. ROCKY STREAM EVENING 42

The GANG has stopped fighting, something is worrying them.

FIDGIT (uncomfortably and unhappily)
Let's make up our minds and get out of here - I don't like it.

RANDALL (surveying the map)
How about Babylon?

WALLY
Who?

RANDALL (scornfully)
You ignorant heap! It's a city of legendary wealth ...

OG (in a strange disembodied, programmed voice)
I got a better idea.

They all turn on the usually amiable, taciturn and innocently dim little OG.

RANDALL
Who said that ?

OG
(his mouth moves strangely, his voice isn't quite his own, it's as if his brain is being manipulated by an outer force)
I got an idea forming ... in my head.

STRUTTER
You haven't had an idea for thousands of years ....

OG (continuing)
There is a place where we could find the greatest thing a man could want ... the goal of everybody's hopes and dreams ..

RANDALL
What are you talking about ?

OG
The Most Fabulous Object in the World ..

They all look interested.

WALLY
That sounds good!

STRUTTER
Yeah.

42 Continued 42

RANDALL
(breaking in)
Hold on!!! We want hard cash, not
some airy-fairy crock of gold nonsense.

STRUTTER
It might be worth a try, Randall.

42A INT. EVIL GENIUS' GROTTO NIGHT 42A

EVIL
They're hooked....greedy little fish.

42B EXT ROCKY STREAM EVENING 42B

OG's voice has merged with EVIL's. It does have a sort of hypnotic effect on the DWARVES. KEVIN notices this.

KEVIN
(quickly)
No! Why does it have to be money we're after
all the time....let's go and find a battle
or a war or something smart like that....

CUT FROM CLOSE UP of KEVIN to

43 INT EVIL GENIUS' GROTTO NIGHT 43

EVIL in his lair.

EVIL
Who is this?

BENSON
I don't know, Your Badness. I've never
seen him before.

EVIL
He is stronger than the rest, who
is he ?

BENSON
I <u>don't</u> ... know..

EVIL
I'm losing them....I'm losing them..
There's something going on down there!

44 EXT. ROCKY STREAM EVENING 44

The GANG are increasingly restless and frightened by this place. The wind has started again. The wind that dares not speak its name. RANDALL is agitatedly looking at the map. WALLY suddenly looks up, over RANDALL's shoulder. His eyes widen.

WALLY
(urgently)
Look Randall!
(he points)
Over there! We'd better move...!

RANDALL
(still preoccupied with planning their route on the map)
Don't rush me!

WALLY
The forest! It's on fire!

RANDALL
It's raining....pudding head!

RANDALL snatches a quick look behind him and double takes.

RANDALL
Oh no....

KEVIN
What is it ?

RANDALL
It's Him...

FIDGIT
It's Him!..

They back away and cower from the growing brightness. The forest does indeed appear to be burning. Scrabbling to try and hide behind each other.

WALLY
He's found us!

FIDGIT
We're done for!

RANDALL
Quick! Make for the hole ... over there!

The glow comes swirling towards them. Wind howls. Trees and bushes are ripped up and thrown through the air. It's impressive and frightening. The GANG fall over each other in their panic, allowing KEVIN to sprint ahead to the hole. The swirling glow coalesces into the shape of the SUPREME BEING. His voice rings out.

44 Continued 44

SUPREME BEING
Stop! I demand you stop! STOP! Now, before it's too late!

RANDALL
(trying to sort the GANG out)
Move it!

In the distance we see KEVIN freeze. He looks back in horror.

KEVIN
(desperately)
There are two holes, Randall! Which one! Which one!

FIDGIT
(screaming above the noise)
Just go!

SUPREME BEING
Do not defy me! Return the map!

KEVIN takes one last despairing look and jumps. As he does so we hear RANDALL scream out.

RANDALL
Not that one, Kevin!

44A INT. EVIL GENIUS' GROTTO NIGHT 44A

EVIL
We've lost them ... !

44B DELETED 44B

PAGES 54/54A/55/56/57 DELETED

45 DELETED 45

46 DELETED 46

47 DELETED 47

48 DELETED 48

49 EXT. MAGNIFICENT LANDSCAPE DAY 49

A pitched battle is in progress on a high barren plain. The sun burns down on distant mountains. A huge WARRIOR - his head and shoulders covered by the rotting head and neck of a bull firmly held in place by heavy leather

49 Continued 49

straps - smashes away with a great club at a helmeted GREEK WARRIOR who defends himself with shield and spear. The BULL-HEAD is the stronger. Dust swirls as they rage back and forth until at last the helmeted WARRIOR is struck down. As he lies on the ground, the BULL-HEAD raises his club for the death blow. But as the club is about to descend KEVIN suddenly drops out of the sky onto the fallen WARRIOR's chest. The BULL-HEAD hesitates, stunned by this sudden interruption. The helmeted WARRIOR grabs this chance to recover his spear and thrust upwards. The BULL-HEADED WARRIOR crashes to the ground dead. KEVIN, who has been thrown to the side, struggles to regain his senses. The helmeted WARRIOR is kneeling over the dead BULL-HEAD. Slowly he turns his attention to KEVIN. He looks terrifying. He starts to approach the BOY. KEVIN tries to scramble away - afraid for his life. The GREEK WARRIOR reaches out and grabs hold of KEVIN's clothes. He pulls KEVIN back.

GREEK WARRIOR
Where did _you_ come from ?

KEVIN
Er... I'm ... not quite sure.

GREEK WARRIOR
Who sent you? The Gods ...?

KEVIN doesn't know what to say ...

GREEK WARRIOR
Zeus? Athena? Apollo....?

KEVIN, rather out of his depth in this Greek mythology rap just stands there speechless.

GREEK WARRIOR
(removing his helmet, revealing himself to be none other than Sean Connery. He grins as only Sean can. (This is the sort of creepy stage direction that helps get the stars interested.)
Well you're certainly a chatty little fellow...

He bends down and retrieves his robe....

KEVIN
(looking at him in amazement)
I don't believe it.

Continued.

49 Continued 49

GREEK WARRIOR
(turns and straightens)
Don't believe what?

KEVIN
Er ... I didn't believe the way you ...
the way you killed him ...

GREEK WARRIOR
(his face clouds)
Yes ... but it has to be done ...
sometimes ...
(he begins to cut off
the bull's head from the
fallen warrior)

KEVIN
No ... No! I meant it was such a
good <u>shot</u> ... you got him right in
the ribs!
(with relish)
I bet you've killed lots of people ...

The GREEK WARRIOR smiles a little distantly ...

GREEK WARRIOR
Hey! The Gods must have given you
a name ...

KEVIN
Who ... <u>me</u>?

The WARRIOR looks round, with a smile. In every direction there is just desert and emptiness.

KEVIN
Oh ... yer ... yes ... Kevin ...

GREEK WARRIOR
(with a hint of bemusement)
Kevin?! D'you want a helmet Kevin?

He holds out his magnificent helmet.

KEVIN
Oh ... oh <u>yes</u> ... yes, please ...

KEVIN holds out his arms to receive the massive helmet, but the GREEK WARRIOR approaches and drops it over KEVIN's head ...

GREEK WARRIOR
(laughing)
It's yours ...

Continued

49 Continued 49

KEVIN
(a muffled, tinny voice from inside)
What ? Mine ?

GREEK WARRIOR
You don't want it ?

KEVIN
(from inside)
Oh yes ... yes please ...You really mean I can have it..

GREEK WARRIOR
.. On condition that you carry it back to the city for me ...

KEVIN finally raises the helmet - with difficulty, for it's heavy and it's hot.

KEVIN
No ... I can't, really ... I er .. I must wait ...
(he looks skywards, briefly)
(lamely)
I'm with some friends ..

The GREEK WARRIOR makes an elaborate play of scanning the desert wastes. He smiles, puzzled.

KEVIN
They'll be meeting me here soon .. You see if I lose them I may never be able to get back ...

GREEK WARRIOR
Get back ... where ?

KEVIN
Er ... I'm not sure ...

49 Continued 49

GREEK WARRIOR shakes his head, smiles and turns.

GREEK WARRIOR
Well..... take this at least.

KEVIN looks quizzical as the WARRIOR slings a skin bag off his shoulder.

GREEK WARRIOR
It's water.... you'll need it.

He takes the helmet back, swings his white horse round and pulls himself up. He stops.

GREEK WARRIOR
Well, whoever you are ... thanks...

He gives him a last look, turns and spurs the horse.

KEVIN
(suddenly deciding)
No...no... I'd like to come please. Please!

The GREEK WARRIOR reins in his horse at the last minute, grins, leans down and pulls KEVIN up onto his fine white stallion. He turns and gallops away.

50 EXT LOOKOUT TOWER DAY 50

A GREEK LOOKOUT stands on an ancient tower. Mountains stretch away in the distance. A great brass horn hangs from a massive tripod. The LOOKOUT is busily polishing the horn. On noticing a distant cloud of dust, he interrupts his labours and peers into the distance. He seems to recognize the RIDER on the white horse. Putting his lips to the horn he lets sound a booming blast.

51 EXT. COUNTRYSIDE DAY 51

The resonating vibrations from the horn reach the GREEK WARRIOR and the BOY. KEVIN's eyes light up. There in the distance stands the city of Mycenae ... a great mud-brick, towering affair. "Mighty impressive!!" T. Gilliam

52 EXT. CITY STREETS DAY 52

The bustle of everyday Mycenean city life is interrupted by the appearance of the WARRIOR and KEVIN on horseback at the far end of the street.

The populace begin to clamour and cheer as they ride up the street.

KEVIN
(shouting)
You're a hero!

GREEK WARRIOR
(smiles)
The warrior we killed was a great enemy of the city ... Many thought they wouldn't see me back here ...

The welcome builds as they wend through the streets.

KEVIN
(shouting over the noise of the crowd)
Where are we going ?

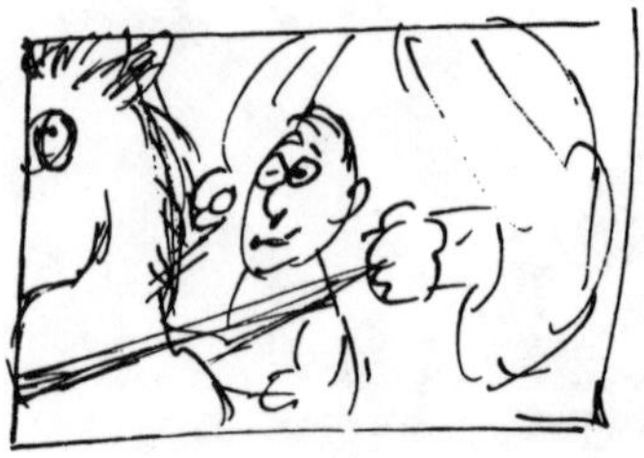

GREEK WARRIOR
To the palace .. We must report to the King ...

KEVIN
King ....! We're going to see a King!

Continued

52 Continued 52

GREEK WARRIOR
He owes me some thanks!

53 EXT. PALACE DAY 53

They reach the gate of the palace. CROWDS form up on either side. They dismount. On a balcony above the gate is a throne, and standing next to it are a QUEEN (CLYTEMNESTRA) and three leading GREEK CITIZENS. The WARRIOR is welcomed by TWO OFFICIALS at the gate. HE BOWS. They bow. Then they lead off - up a flight of steps inside the gate. Again the WARRIOR beckons to KEVIN to follow him. KEVIN does a real "who ... me?" and tries to back away ... The GREEK WARRIOR grabs him by the arm.

54 INT. PALACE STEPS DAY

He leads him up the steps.

KEVIN
(to Greek Warrior)
Which one is the King?

GREEK WARRIOR
He hasn't arrived yet. Everyone has to wait for him.

55 EXT. PALACE BALCONY DAY 55

They reach the balcony at the top of the steps. CLYTEMNESTRA and her THREE BUDDIES from the Justice Department smile icily. The crowd fall silent. KEVIN looks round expectantly. The WARRIOR turns to the CROWD and raises the bull's head. Noticing KEVIN has shrunk back he whispers loudly to him and motions with his head for KEVIN to stand next to him.

GREEK WARRIOR
You saved my life, remember.

Then with a mighty fling, he hurls the bull's head into the crowd.

GREEK WARRIOR
The enemy is dead..! long live the freedom of the city!

Great horn booms out.

CROWD
Hail the King! Hail the King!

KEVIN
(tugging WARRIOR's sleeve)
The King! He's coming!

55 Continued 55

KEVIN looks round but can see nobody. He looks back to the WARRIOR. Suddenly the drachma drops and young KEVIN realizes what we've all dug at least 6 reels earlier - that his Soul Buddy in the warrior suit is THE MAN.

LEADING CITIZEN
Hail King Agamemnon!

KEVIN's jaw drops

CROWD
(answering)
Hail King Agamemnon!

AGAMEMNON looks down at KEVIN and winks with a broad grin. KEVIN looks up to him. Reassured. This is KEVIN's greatest moment so far ... (but read on, Great Moment spotters)...

CROWD
Hail .... Agamemnon.

56 INT. PALACE DAY 56

CUT TO a frieze depicting a naval battle in Greek times. It depicts quite a juicy scene of carnage.

PULL OUT to reveal it's on the wall of a room in Agamemnon's palace. KEVIN is peering at it with interest.

KEVIN
There's a man getting cut in half here. It must have been a brilliant battle...

AGAMEMNON sits at a table: he is reading a scroll and discussing with an ADVISER, he seems pre-occupied and deeply bugged by the vagaries of destiny.

AGAMEMNON
All four are to receive summary executions today ... if she wishes to see me, I shall be at the courts in the afternoon.

ADVISER bows and leaves. At the door AGAMEMNON calls him:

AGAMEMNON
I still rule this city, Thersites. Tell the Queen that.

Continued.

56 Continued 56

ADVISER
Sir ...

He bows and leaves. AGAMEMNON starts to unroll a scroll with naval designs thereon.

KEVIN
I wish I'd been in the Trojan Wars ...
seen Priam and Hector ... and all
those javelins flying and swordfights ...

AGAMEMNON looks up from his work. He smiles.

KEVIN
Will you show me how to sword-
fight ...? Please ...

AGAMEMNON
Come here, I'll show you something
much more useful ...

KEVIN crosses to the table. AGAMEMNON pulls over a couple of goblets and motions to KEVIN to fetch another.

AGAMEMNON
Bring one of those ...

KEVIN puts the goblet on the table. AGAMEMNON turns two upside down, then puts a round red paperweight under the third and turns it upside down. He juggles them around.

AGAMEMNON
Now ... where is it?

KEVIN
(after some
consideration)
That one ...

KING turns it up, nothing there. KEVIN shakes his head and points to the next. KING turns it up, nothing there, with a sigh of resignation KEVIN turns up the other .. it's not there. AGAMEMNON grins and produces it from KEVIN's ear.

KEVIN
Kings aren't supposed to do things
like that!

AGAMEMNON laughs and gets up.

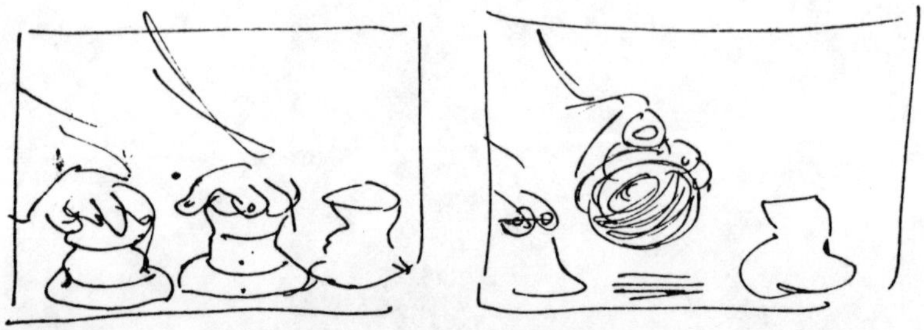

57 EXT. CITY WALLS DAY 57

AGAMEMNON and KEVIN accompanied by GUARDS walk through a garden along the base of the towering walls of the city. FRUIT PICKERS and GARDENERS are at work.

KEVIN
But I thought King Agamemnon was always fighting ... he was a warrior.

AGAMEMNON
(face clouds)
Mmmm ... but when you're <u>not</u> fighting that's the good time ... that's when you have time to learn things ... like how to use one of these ...

AGAMEMNON pulls his knife from its sheath. It's very simple but beautiful. He hands it to KEVIN.

KEVIN
and I'll be able to kill Trojans ...
(he starts to mock stab at a FRUIT PICKER)

AGAMEMNON
(bellowing)
No!
(he grabs the knife from Kevin's hand, cutting himself in the process)
Don't ever do that ... never in fun.
(noticing blood on his hand he calms down)
There are better uses like ... er ... slicing apples ...

KEVIN
(a little scornfully)
Slicing <u>apples</u>!

AGAMEMNON picks up a couple of apples from a pallet ... throws them to one of the GUARDS, and indicates with his head to the GUARD to throw them. The GUARD tosses an apple up; quick as a flash AGAMEMNON's blade whips through the air and impales the apple and embeds it in the trunk of a tree. There is a pause. then it falls neatly in two halves onto the ground. KEVIN's jaw drops. AGAMEMNON goes across, picks up the apple halves, takes a bite of one, and tosses the other to KEVIN. He grins broadly as KEVIN examines the apple in cautious wonderment.

AGAMEMNON
Do you like apples?

57 Continued 57

KEVIN
Mmmm...yes...

AGAMEMNON pulls his knife from the tree, and holds it out to the BOY.

AGAMEMNON
Then it's yours.

57A DELETED 57A

58 EXT. PALACE BALCONY EVENING 58

In the dying rays of the evening sun the PEOPLE of Mycenae go about their business - donkeys laden with baskets push past playing CHILDREN. The CAMERA PULLS BACK to reveal KEVIN leaning over the edge of the balcony, taking a Polaroid picture. He then turns and takes a snap of AGAMEMNON who is discussing something with one of his officials. KEVIN turns back to the view over the city and watches the picture develop.

KEVIN
You know .... I never ever want to go back.

AGAMEMNON
Don't you want to see all your friends again?

KEVIN
(grimaces)
No....no.... thanks....

AGAMEMNON
Don't you want to be in your own home...?

KEVIN
(less convinced, but after a moment's pause)
....No...

58 Continued 58

AGAMEMNON
... to be with your own father...
your own mother...?

KEVIN looks down at his half-finished Greek writing, looks up and out of the window, over the city, to the flourishing plain and in the distance the glittering blue sea, he looks back to AGAMEMNON:

KEVIN
....No...

AGAMEMNON
Then....

KEVIN
I can stay!

AGAMEMNON
No more questions. To bed and sleep well. I may have a surprise for you tomorrow...

KEVIN stands eagerly.

KEVIN
What sort of surprise ?

AGAMEMNON
Wait till tomorrow...

They shake hands solemnly. KEVIN suddenly frowns.

KEVIN
It won't...It won't suddenly go away ... all this, will it...?

AGAMEMNON
I said ... no more questions ...
(but he smiles)

KEVIN smiles and runs off. At the door he waves, then reaches behind his ear and produces - the red paperweight. He gives a grin of triumph.

AGAMEMNON
That's good!

KEVIN heaves a great big proud, happy smile and throws the ball to AGAMEMNON.

59 INT. KEVIN'S ROOM MORNING 59

KEVIN's room in the castle at Mycenae, next morning. KEVIN wakes. The sun is streaming through. A marvellous day, a superb, clear blue-skied, gentle-breezed, soft, sweet-smelling Mediterranean morning, the like of which only exists in the minds of half-crazed Englishmen writing in Kentish Town, London, NW5, in January.

Continued

59 Continued 59

Slowly KEVIN's eyes focus on the room. His expression suddenly changes. There towering over him are two priests in terrifying-looking masks. One of them holds in his hands a blindfold that he thrusts down towards the CAMERA. Blackness.

60 INT. PASSAGEWAY DAY 60

The PRIESTS lead KEVIN, blindfolded, along a passageway. Much activity is going around them ... Preparation for some important event.

KEVIN
What are you doing... where are you taking me?

HEAD PRIEST
These are King Agamemnon's instructions.

61 INT. PALACE COURTYARD DAY 61

KEVIN is led out into a brilliant sunlit courtyard. ATTENDANTS fuss around him. He is lifted up. The blindfold is removed. He finds himself mounted upon a magnificent horse with beautiful golden wings rising from its breastplate. A rich robe has been put around KEVIN and on his head is a gold headdress. The horse canters around the courtyard. The ATTENDANTS bow. One of the COURT OFFICIALS motions to KEVIN to guide the horse through the doorway into the Palace Hall. KEVIN does so.

62 INT. PALACE HALL DAY 62

KEVIN enters the hall on his magnificent winged horse. There is the entire court assembled. AGAMEMNON motions KEVIN over to the royal throne. Next to it is a smaller throne. KEVIN is seated on it. Then he is showered with wondrous golden gifts. AGAMEMNON rises and holds up his hand for silence.

AGAMEMNON
I have decreed that this boy shall remain here with us in our city. Furthermore, hear you all now and let is be known abroad that he shall be from this day forward my own son. Heir to the throne of Mycenae!

KEVIN can hardly believe it. AGAMEMNON turns to one of his ADVISERS who gives him a gold-leaf crown which AGAMEMNON lays on KEVIN's head. Around his waist is strapped a beautiful gold knife. He grasps him by the arm, and presents KEVIN to the PEOPLE.

AGAMEMNON
Now let the banquet begin....

Cheers, applause, food is brought in, followed by wine.

62 Continued 62

A great, spitted roast ox is brought in. Oohs and Ah's. A shaven-headed brute of a MAN (Amos Beefcake by name) raises a golden sword, and splits the ox in two. To the delight of the AUDIENCE, fruit tumbles out - mangoes, pert little peaches, oranges etc. As they sit, KEVIN is still lost in sheer delight and pleasure.

KEVIN
You really mean I shall stay here for ever ...

AGAMEMNON nods with a smile.

AGAMEMNON
(suddenly serious)
in return, you must promise to remember all I taught you. Choose your friends with care, and never -

His speech is interrupted by a drum roll and flourish of tambourines. The KING turns and smiles ...

AGAMEMNON
Now ... enjoy yourself ...
(he claps his hands)

All heads turn as the ENTERTAINERS appear. They are three MASKED FIGURES with false horse heads jutting from their middles ... like mounted riders. They cavort about the hall to the sounds of drum and pipe. People laugh. Some clap ... general enjoyment. KEVIN is in 17th heaven. Suddenly they come apart. Each FIGURE becomes two SMALL FIGURES - one masked, the other horse-headed. In all there are SIX TINY FIGURES. KEVIN has a sudden attack of horrified realisation which is quickly confirmed when the FIGURES start dancing around him. One by one they lift their masks so that only he can get a glimpse of their faces. They are none other than the DWARVES. They all wink knowingly at him. KEVIN doesn't know what to do. Madly the DWARVES cavort around him - whispering their pride in his wonderful scheme.

RANDALL
Good work, Kevin .... <u>very</u> good work.

FIDGIT
Sorry we took so long to find you ...

Continued

62 Continued 62

They try to pull him up from his throne. He clings to it, but the CROWD, loving the DWARVES' antics, encourage the BOY to join in. The BOY looks desperately to AGAMEMNON, but he too is encouraging the BOY to enjoy himself and to relax. The BOY is lifted from the throne and bundled into the middle of the great hall and on to a platform.

STRUTTER
We make a good team, eh ... you set it up ... we come in just at the right moment.

The DWARVES seem to be preparing a wondrous magic trick for they have gathered together all the riches they can manage - even to the extent of asking for jewellery - which is freely given by the happy expectant AUDIENCE. One of the DWARVES is anxiously eyeing his watch. The BOY tries helplessly to escape - he knows what is about to happen. The AUDIENCE is howling with laughter. The KING is enjoying the spectacle immensely. But the DWARVES hold

Continued

62 Continued 62

the BOY firmly. They think he is trying to go back for more booty. Unfortunately time is up. Reaching down, the DWARVES lift up a ring of cloth that encloses them and the riches. The BOY, the DWARVES and the goodies are gone. The CROWD applauds madly.

63 EXT OCEANLINER DAY 63

An ocean liner, circa 1912. Steaming along in stately fashion ...

64 EXT LINER'S DECK (FIRST CLASS) DAY 64

TWO COUPLES in period costume, cigarette holders, etc. wander by. Another YOUNG COUPLE - he in white flannels, cravat - she in tennis gear - come TOWARDS CAMERA and, leaning on the rail, they stare out to sea. The music plays in the background. They've just met and they are in love. They are still called VINCENT and PANSY.

He turns to her adoringly...

VINCENT
At last ... we're alone.

PANSY
(looking out to sea)
Isn't it glorious.

VINCENT
I love the ocean.... God,I love her ..
She's so .... so ...

PANSY
Wet ?

VINCENT
Yes ... so ... so damn ... wet ..
yes ...

PAUSE. VINCENT executes an incredibly nimble 4-step pas-de-deux (without falling over) and pulls her to him.

VINCENT
Pansy, look at me.

PANSY
(looking up shyly)
Yes, Vincent.

VINCENT
Do you ... do you ... love me ?

64 Continued 64

PANSY
Of course I love you.

VINCENT
You ... you don't mind the thing ...
on my ... on my nose ...

PANSY
Oh you mean your ,..

VINCENT
Yes my -

PANSY
No darling ... of course I don't mind ...

VINCENT
You could get used to having a chap
around the house with a ... with a
.. with a damn thing on his nose.

PANSY
Of course my love. Everyone has something
odd about them ... I 've got an enormous -

VINCENT
Pansy, I'm so glad you feel like that,
because now at last I can ask you ...

PANSY
Oh ask me ... ask me ...

VINCENT
Will you ? Oh, Pansy will you -

Suddenly with a cry and a shriek six DWARF BANDITS, KEVIN and all the Greek treasures rip through the awning over their heads and fall on top of them. She screams. He shouts. There is pandemonium. Shouts of "My hairpiece! Save my hairpiece!"

WALLY
Where the hell are we ...

VINCENT
(struggling up from behind them)
Damn you ...

PANSY
Save me Vincent ... Vincent!

We see for the first time her POV. Pansy screams and runs off. VINCENT is revealed to be bald.

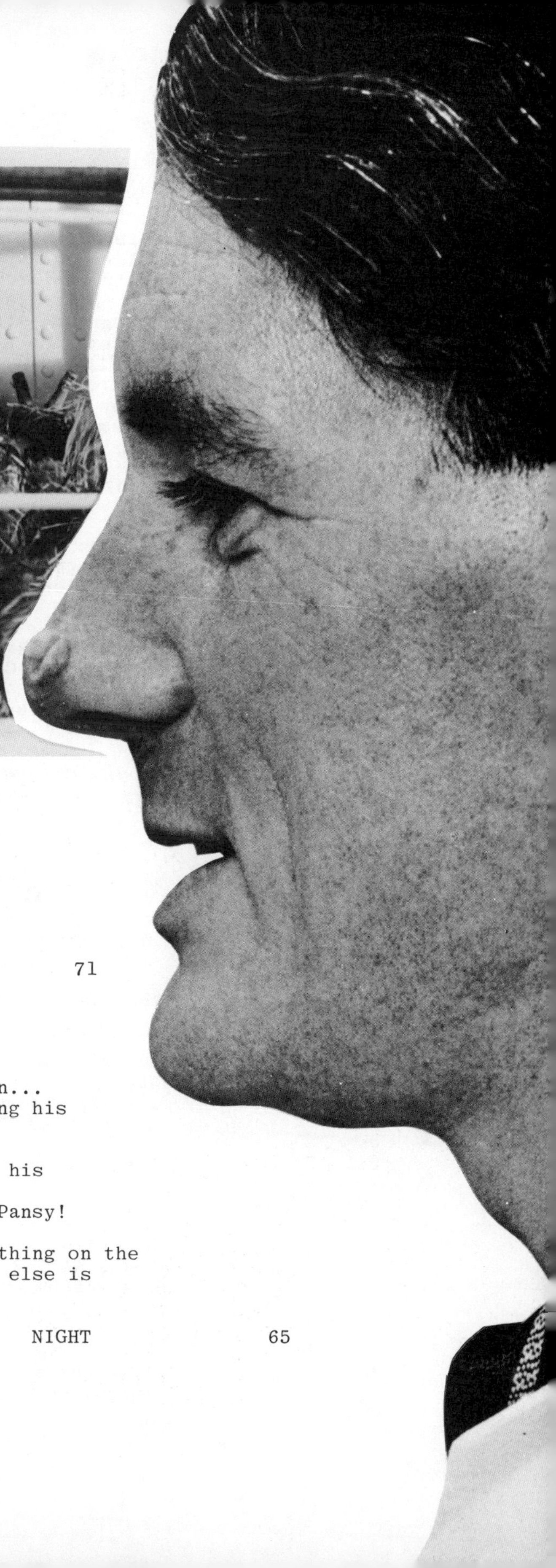

64 Continued

VINCENT
(grabbing toupée)
Pansy ! Pansy, I can explain...
(to VERMIN who is eating his hairpiece)
Give me that.
(he tries to put it on his head)
You've ruined everything! Pansy!
(he runs off shouting)
It's only the hair and the thing on the nose, honestly! Everything else is fine?

65 EXT. LINER'S DECK (VERY FIRST CLASS) NIGHT 65

65 Continued 65

COUPLES in evening dress, cigarette holders, etc., wander by. In the background waltzing COUPLES are seen in silhouette through the ballroom windows as an orchestra plays somewhere OUT OF SHOT. We TRACK WITH COUPLES and pick up KEVIN in the foreground staring disconsolately out to sea. He is dressed in smart new period clothes. Behind him, in a row of deckchairs, recline the GANG dressed to the nines in tuxedos and bow ties. They are glittering with gold rings, flash wristwatches and pomaded hair. Each of them smokes a fat cigar. Champagne bottles are being emptied. We TIGHTEN IN ON THEM.

VERMIN is speaking to a WAITER.

VERMIN
6 plates of caviar please ... oh ...
(he turns to the others)
Anyone else want any ?

WALLY
No I'll stick to the quail's eyeballs, thank you. Caviar makes me throw up.

RANDALL throws WALLY a sharply disapproving glance.

WALLY
(quickly, apologetically)
Sorry ... sorry, Randall.

OG burps loudly, they all turn on him.

RANDALL
(calling out to KEVIN)
Cheer up Kevin! Kings aren't the only ones with money.

KEVIN
The money wasn't important.

RANDALL
And you know why, Kevin, he was stuck in Ancient Greece and he didn't have anything to spend it on.

KEVIN (turning away bitterly)
You make me sick!

Much mock horror amongst the reclining DWARVES, then laughter. RANDALL, after an exchange of looks with the others, gets up and approaches KEVIN, very niftily picking a champagne cocktail off the tray of a WAITER bending low to the next table as he does so. He leans on the rail beside KEVIN in avuncular fashion.

RANDALL
(munching on his cigar)
I've got something to tell you Kevin ..

65 Continued 65

KEVIN
Go away!

RANDALL
It's about the map!

KEVIN
(bitterly)
The map! I don't understand you, Randall .. You have something like that map - something really brilliant, that gives you all this power, and you're just wasting it.

RANDALL
(a little indignantly)
I don't call this wasting it ...
(he nods around at the liner, the champagne and all the trappings)
... I mean this isn't all bad eh ... This isn't all bad at all ..

KEVIN
Why couldn't you leave me where I was happy....

RANDALL
(looking around with exaggerated caution, then speaking close and confidentially to KEVIN, his eyes suddenly alight with enthusiasm)
Because you're going to be a lot happier when you hear what we've got planned ...
(he leans even further in)
I was having a close look at the map last night, and you know what I found....?
(impressive pause)
Og was right ...
(another impressive pause)
.. the Most Fabulous Object in the World... it does exist!

He looks at KEVIN, waiting for a reaction that doesn't come. KEVIN just shakes his head wearily. RANDALL puts his glass on the rail, and eyes an elderly VICAR who happens to be taking the air right beside him, with such malevolence that he moves rather quickly away. RANDALL then produces the map.

65 Continued 65

RANDALL
(urgently, excited)
We've been looking in all the obvious places ... but ... look ... down here ... there's a place called The Time of Legends ... it's sort of outside time as we know it ... giants, wizards, all that ... here in the middle of The Time of Legends - the Fortress of Ultimate Darkness - and inside the Fortress of Ultimate Darkness - the Most Fabulous Object in the World.

Someone walks by. RANDALL hastily puts the map away.

KEVIN
The Time of Legends! It doesn't exist.

RANDALL
It does exist ... if you believe in it Kevin. If you really believe in it. Otherwise Horseflesh wouldn't have put it on the map.

KEVIN
T...ch!
(he turns away dismissively)

RANDALL
(after a quick glance at the other DWARVES who are now singing drukenly and occasionally whistling at a bit of high-class passing tail)

You know, you and me have a lot in common, Kevin ... we like a risk .. we like adventure .. well this is it, Kevin. This is the Ultimate Adventure. None of your namby-pamby Time Holes to mess around with here... This is the Big One! We stake all... we win everything.

KEVIN
I've just lost everything ... because of you.

RANDALL
All right! I know how you feel ... But there's no hurry yet ... just think about it though ... and remember Kevin ... whatever you think of me, I did get you all this.

He indicates all the luxury around.

65 Continued

RANDALL
(beckons)
Waiter!

CUT TO TWO WAITERS. One looks over to RANDALL.

RANDALL
(expansively)
More champagne.

WAITER
Of course sir ...

He walks briskly off, revealing a large sign "S.S. TITANIC" behind him and his colleague.

RANDALL
And lots of ice!

65 Continued 65

At that moment there is a rending crunch ... screams off, a moment's pause, and then the deck tilts at a 45° angle and the BANDITS still holding cigars and champagne glasses slide gracefully out of sight. VINCENT and PANSY slide by.

66 EXT. TITANIC SINKING NIGHT 66

CUT TO SHOT of the liner, tilted up and sinking. Shouts, screams, calls of "Abandon Ship!" Horns and hooters going. Over it all we hear a throttled voice.

VINCENT
I can explain <u>everything</u>, Pansy.

67 EXT SEA NIGHT 67

CUT TO THE SIX BANDITS & KEVIN all hanging forlornly onto the big wooden sign "S.S. TITANIC" - this is about eight feet long and can accommodate them all. Pieces of iceberg float by. FIDGIT is hysterical.

FIDGIT
I want to go home ... I can't stand it. You'll get us all killed Randall!

RANDALL
Shut up Fidgit! I didn't know we were going to run slap-bang into an iceberg! It didn't say on the ticket "get off before the iceberg!"

STRUTTER
I suppose it's silly asking where the ..... the rest of the loot is ...

RANDALL
(slightly hysterically)
It's safe ... Strutter ... absolutely safe in a specially locked strong-box ... Here is the key... 017 ... As soon as they raise the Titanic I'll be the first one on board. Stop eating this plank, Vermin... !

VERMIN is nibbling the end of the spar on which their life depends.

FIDGIT
(forlornly)
Help! Help!

67 Continued 67

WALLY
Help!

These pathetic cries hang on the night air.

The evil wind blows over the floating spar. OG's eyes glaze.

OG
(in his strange voice)
Now is the time to begin our quest for the Most Fabulous Object, Randall.

RANDALL
Og's right! We've still got the map. Let's go.

WALLY
What?...Randall, we're in the middle of the Atlantic Ocean!

RANDALL
They have time-holes in the middle of oceans!

FIDGIT
You're crazy.

RANDALL
You've just got to trust me.

FIDGIT
That's the problem!

RANDALL
Trust Horseflesh! He made the map... he wouldn't have put the Land of Legends on if it didn't exist!

STRUTTER & WALLY
You could be right!

FIDGIT
You're crazy!

RANDALL
(screaming over the storm)
We must try !

KEVIN
No!

RANDALL
Altogether now! Abandon plank!

He does so, then STRUTTER and WALLY, and OG, beaming because he doesn't know what's going on. FIDGIT looking terrified.

FIDGIT
I can't swim!

67 Continued 67

He slips off the plank. Only KEVIN remains clinging on. He looks on in horror as FIDGIT gurgles and thrashes in the water. KEVIN has to help him.

KEVIN
I'm coming, Fidgit! I'll save you.

So KEVIN lets go of the plank .. it drifts away. All the DWARVES are starting to panic and scream and thrash about.

KEVIN
Randall! You're mad!

But at that moment a whirlpool forms and travels towards them faster and faster. They can't stay afloat, they're being sucked down ... mocking laughter mixes with their screams.

68 INT. EVIL'S GROTTO DAY 68

EVIL is gloating over their desperate plight.

Applause from all EVIL's minions ...

EVIL
Now we have them ...

ROBERT
Oh well done, Your Viciousness ... !

EVIL
(laughing his deep and sinister laugh)
Suddenly I feel very, very good.

BENSON
(understandingly)
I'm sorry, Master.

EVIL
It'll pass ... Robert!

BENSON
(with malevolent excitement)
Can I bring them in, Master ?

EVIL
Yes, Benson, bring them in to the Time of Legends.

69 DELETED 69

70 DELETED 70

71 DELETED 71

72 DELETED 72

73 DELETED 73

74 DELETED 74

75 DELETED 75

76 EXT. MISTY SEA DAY 76

CUT TO boiling watery surface. The water is bunching itself up. With a great whoosh it spits out one of the GANG - high into the air. He arcs through the mist and then splashes back into the sea. Whoosh - two more DWARVES catapult out of the sea and fly through the air. Another and then another make their appearance. Whoosh. Splash. Whoosh. Splash. Spluttering and thrashing about in the water they become aware of a change in their appearance. Their black evening dress has somehow changed colour - they are now dressed all in white. They look around a bit dismayed.

FIDGIT is struggling, then suddenly eases. They all look round a bit fearfully.

FIDGIT
Hey! I can swim ..

OG
(pointing into the distance)
Look ...

There in the mist-shrouded distance is a strange evil-looking boat languidly listing its way across the sea.

FIDGIT
(frightened but hopeful)
A friendly boat ?

76 Continued 76

RANDALL
(with half-hearted optimism)
Yeah... probably ... Hello!
Hello!

77 INT. OGRE'S CABIN DAY 77

CUT TO twitching of a horrid, hairy, clawed hand lying on a dirty pillow in a darkened cabin. It opens and closes with animal-like snores. A door opens and a FIGURE enters the cabin. A window is opened and a shaft of light falls upon the hand. With a start the hand awakes. It stretches and then proceeds to scratch around in the bedclothes. A WOMAN is preparing a potion by the window of the low-ceilinged cabin.

MRS OGRE
Morning dear.

A distant cry from the dwarves. "Hello!"

OGRE
What was that?

MRS OGRE
What ... dear?

OGRE
I thought I heard a noise ....

MRS OGRE
No... it's your nerves, dear.

The owner of the hand, a horrifying ugly OGRE, climbs out of bed grumbling and whining.

OGRE
...Ooh ... eurggh...
(and various other subhuman
mumblings and grunts)

His WIFE comes across and gives him medicine. He drinks it. And shakes his head ... she hands him a jar of cream.

MRS OGRE
And the ointment for the leg...

He takes it and rubs it on, occasionally wincing with the effort. She goes to the side and starts to prepare a steaming draught.

77 Continued 77

OGRE

Oooh ... aaagh ... oooh ...
(he really is in bad shape)
I grew too fast when I was young, that was the problem....

MRS. OGRE

(bringing over the steaming potion)
And ... inhale!

She holds an inhalant in front of him.

OGRE

(moaning)
I can't inhale, it's bad for my back.

77 Continued 77

MRS. OGRE
It's good for your throat, dear,
come on ...

With some wincing he moves across. Sniffs through one nostril, then another.

OGRE
I wouldn't have these sore throats
if I wasn't an ogre ...

MRS. OGRE
You've been overdoing it, that's all.

He puts his leg up and she starts to apply ointment to the knee very deftly.

OGRE
You try being beastly and terrifying
when you can only get one hour's sleep
a night because your back hurts and
you daren't cough in case you pull a
muscle.

MRS. OGRE
(tenderly, reassuringly)
You're horrible, dear ...

OGRE
You're just saying that.

MRS. OGRE

(she holds out a glass)
Gargle!

He knocks back the mouthwash (gargle) and gargles (mouthwashes) with a roaring, rumbling appalling roar ..

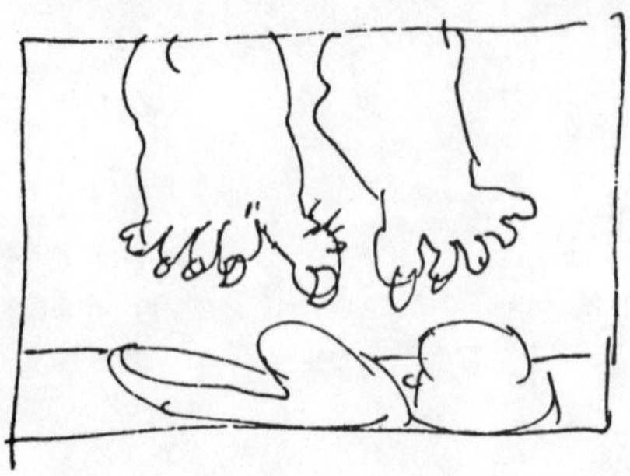

78 EXT. MISTY SEA DAY 78

CUT TO misty sea. The DWARVES and KEVIN are swimming towards the boat. They're suddenly transfixed by the unearthly sound of the gargler (mouthwasher).

STRUTTER
What's that ?

RANDALL
I don't know.

FIDGIT
Come on!

They then try to swim the other way, frantically....

79 INT. OGRE'S CABIN DAY 79

CUT BACK to the boat. OGRE picks up a large net and lumbers out of the door. Just as he is about to go out, he catches sight of himself in a mirror. He stops and puts his face close to the glass.

OGRE
(despondenly)
Look at these spots!

MRS OGRE
You'll grow out of them, dear....

She busies herself at the medecine chest.

80 EXT OGRE'S BOAT DAY 80

CUT TO him emerging onto the deck of the boat, which we now see is on the misty sea.

OGRE
(bitterly)
That's diet that is. All this bloody fish....

80A EXT. MISTY SEA DAY 80A

CUT TO DWARVES swimming away like mad.

80B EXT. OGRE'S BOAT DAY 80B

The OGRE starts to get his net ready, grumbling the while.

OGRE
There used to be a time when you
could be sure of catching old
boots, cans, hatracks, boxes, .,
now it's prawns all the bloody time ..
Anti-pollution!
(he spits into the sea)

He hurls the net out wincing as he does so. It splashes in the distance.

There is a cry... the net stiffens and pulls. He hangs on ... more shrieks ..

80B Continued 80B

OGRE
(shouting into the cabin)
Wife!

81 INT. OGRE'S CABIN DAY 81

MRS OGRE
(grinding up dried feet
in a meat grinder)
What d'you want dear .... the foot powder?

OGRE
No ... come out here and help me ... quick!

She puts down the mortar and pestle and hurries out.

82 EXT. OGRE'S BOAT DAY 82

He's trying to pull the heavy net in despite of lumbar problems. Noise and struggles from the net.

MRS OGRE
What's in there!

OGRE
(grinning)
I don't know but it's not <u>prawns</u> ... oww!

MRS OGRE
Leave it to me ... dear, please....

She grabs the net and with easy superhuman strength, heaves the net out ... inside the net are the DWARVES and KEVIN, packed inside with lots of fish.

MRS OGRE
Oh, aren't they lovely?

The crushed up, bedraggled and shivering DWARVES are somewhat encouraged by this kindly LADY. They smile weakly up at her.

82 Continued 82

MRS OGRE
We can have them for breakfast!

The DWARVES' smiles fade.

OGRE
(eyes lighting up)
You mean - eat their boots !

MRS OGRE
No dear...Eat all of them!..
every bit....that's what Ogres
do, dear....

OGRE
(his eyes lighting up)
Yes...yes! Of course....

MRS OGRE
We could have them grilled....

OGRE
(doubtful)
Yes...yes....

MRS OGRE
Or minced with a side salad ?
- No, you don't like salads, do you..?

OGRE
Nothing in them....

MRS OGRE
I know - fondue!...
We haven't had a fondue for years...
we'll need the big pot and skewers..

She makes to bustle off.

Panic reactions from the DWARVES throughout this.

OGRE
(after her, anxiously)
What shall I do....dear ..-?

MRS OGRE
(aside, to him)
Terrify them.....

OGRE
What about my back ?

MRS OGRE
You don't have to jump around, just
about horribly....and leer at them....
you know...like you used to do.

82 Continued 82

MRS OGRE disappears ... muttering cheerfully ... "Oh this is wonderful".

OGRE
Right....

OGRE goes back to them and goes into a very unconvincing OGRE routine - lots of grimaces, evil "HA! HA! HA's" and close peerings into their faces.

OGRE
Now ... let me see what we have here ...
Ha! Ha! some tasty little morsels eh?
Ooo!

He winces in pain as he kneels down and starts to open the net and retrieve the terrified DWARVES ... He grabs FIDGIT.

82 Continued 82

and puts him into a cooking pot. FIDGIT screams. OGRE winces, and grabs his back.

OGRE
(manfully)
Eh eh! Eh .... Fee! Fi! Fo!
Fu- ow!.

A really bad spasm hits him just as he grabs KEVIN.

KEVIN
(terrified)
D...d...does your back ... er ...
hurt?
(trying one final shot)
I know a cure for bad backs...

OGRE
Bad back? Me ? An Ogre ?
Ha, ha ... oh! aargh!

KEVIN
What you need is stretching.

OGRE
Stretching?

KEVIN
A man stretched my father once,
and he never had any trouble.

OGRE
Ha! Ha!

KEVIN
We could do it for you.

OGRE
Certainly NOT! Ow!

83 DELETED 83

84 DELETED 84

PAGE 87 DELETED

85 INT. OGRE'S CABIN DAY

MRS OGRE is cheerfully preparing some vicious looking knives and long skewers, making sure they're the right length for each DWARF. She is singing her fondue song.

(lilting)

Oh, it's wonderful, yes it's wonderful
To be making fondue again.
To be melting the cheese in a southerly breeze
To be sharpening the skewers and then
Sticking little men on the end of them
And sitting down at a table for two
Enjoying the moonlight, the stars and the dish
That the French-speaking Swiss call fondue.

It's cheap and it's good
Better for you than wood,
Rubber tyres, iron filings or glue
You can lick, you can nibble
You can dip in and dribble
You can suck it then bite it in two..
Oh! Life on board ship goes so well with the dip
That the French-speaking Swiss call fondue.

Oh! I'm so happy, yes I'm so happy
I'll be eating my fondue tonight
I'll be singing my song while suspending my prong
Over pure gastronomic delight
Then I'll let it drop, with a sticky plop
In the foaming mass of cheese stew
That the shepherds, the cowherds, religious thinkers (such
as Calvin and Zwingli) and all
Of the French-speaking Swiss call fondue...

Oh! I'm so happy ... oh it's wonderful ...etc etc

She whistles happily ... suddenly she hears a sharp groan from outside ... she looks up.

86 EXT. OGRE'S BOAT DAY 86

The OGRE is flat out, stretched on deck. KEVIN and RANDALL/WALLY have one arm each, FIDGIT and STRUTTER one leg, OG and VERMIN the other ...

KEVIN

And heave....

They pull the OGRE apart.

OGRE

AARGHHH!
(then he smiles)
That's better! That's better!
That's wonderful.......

86A INT. OGRE'S CABIN DAY 86A

MRS OGRE

Are they in the pot yet? Dear?

86B EXT OGRE'S BOAT DAY 86B

OGRE
Yes, just about....

KEVIN and RANDALL
And one more for luck...Heave!
(he winks at Randall)
One two....

They start to swing the OGRE to the right, then they swing the OGRE to the left......

KEVIN and RANDALL
...right....left....right....

OGRE
Hey....what's going on......?

KEVIN
Left....right....left....right
...and over!

OGRE
Aaaaaarghh.....!

They swing the yelling OGRE overboard, he disappears into the viscous oily sea.

MRS. OGRE
(shouting from inside)
What's going on ?

KEVIN
(to GANG)
Quick! Get in the pot!

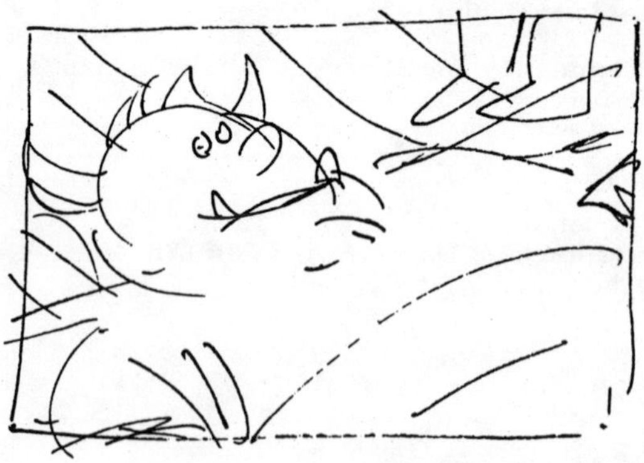

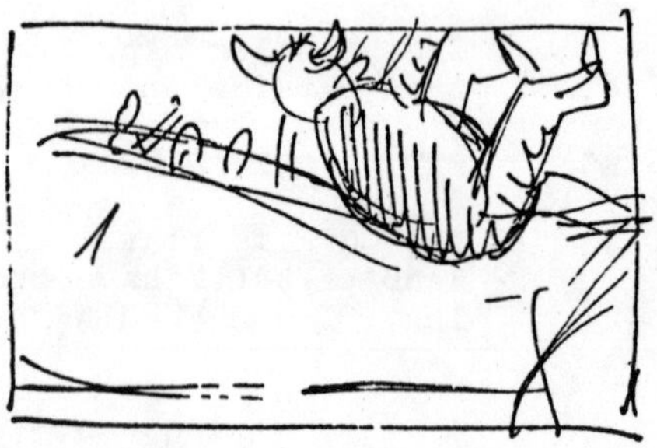

86B Continued 86B

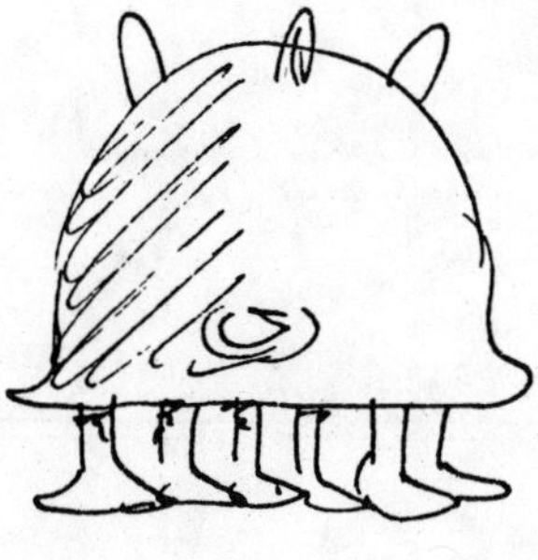

FIDGIT
(in high alarm)
Get in the pot!

KEVIN
Don't ask questions!
(They all jump into the cooking pot. In the water ...)

OGRE
(surfacing)
Is this part of the cure?!

87 INT OGRE'S CABIN DAY 87

MRS OGRE, running her finger along the edge of the knife.

MRS OGRE
Are you alright dear!
(no reply)
Winston? Winston!

88 EXT. OGRE'S BOAT DAY 88

She runs out of the door and up on to deck. She looks round, can't see anyone. She crosses to the deck rail, and sees him.

MRS OGRE
Winston! What are you doing in the water? .. ow!

At that moment the large black cooking pot behind her begins rocking back and forth and then with a lurch it flips over supported by 7 pairs of feet and waddles speedily across the deck and pushes her backside tipping her over into the water.

Then the pot is lifted off revealing the DWARVES and KEVIN. They peer over the side.

89 EXT. MISTY SEA DAY 89

MRS OGRE
(spluttering from the water)
I've never had a meal treat me like that before! Winston ... we must stop them.

OGRE
Oh! My back is wonderful ... I've never felt so free ..

MRS OGRE
Winston! Get after them!

89 Continued 89

OGRE (with a huge smile
of happiness and relief)

And I can cough! At last I can really
cough.

He gives a mighty cough of such force that a huge noise shatters the atmosphere, and the sail fills with wind and the boat is borne away ...

90 EXT. OGRE'S BOAT DAY 90

KEVIN
(as the boat careers
out of shot)
Quick! The rudder!

He and RANDALL make a grab for the rudder as the boat sails away.

CUT TO a shot of the boat fairly moving along. They look back. Dim sounds of the OGRE sneezing and coughing recede into the distance.

90A EXT. OGRE'S BOAT DAY 90A

Later. STRUTTER and RANDALL are at the rudder. OG and KEVIN are lashing sail to the boom. VERMIN has a huge box of fish and hands some out, raw, to KEVIN, WALLY and FIDGIT.

WALLY
(turning down a raw
fish and clambering up
a ratline)
How're we doing, Randall?

RANDALL is peering ahead through a telescope. The boat is making good progress, but it's still rather unreal.

RANDALL
Just fine. So long as this wind
keeps up there's not much can go wrong ...

Suddenly the boat lurches violently from side to side. FIDGIT, KEVIN, OG and VERMIN and the fish are all thrown on top of each other and they slide and slither in a heap against the port rail.

RANDALL
Strutter! Keep the rudder straight!

STRUTTER
It _is_ straight!

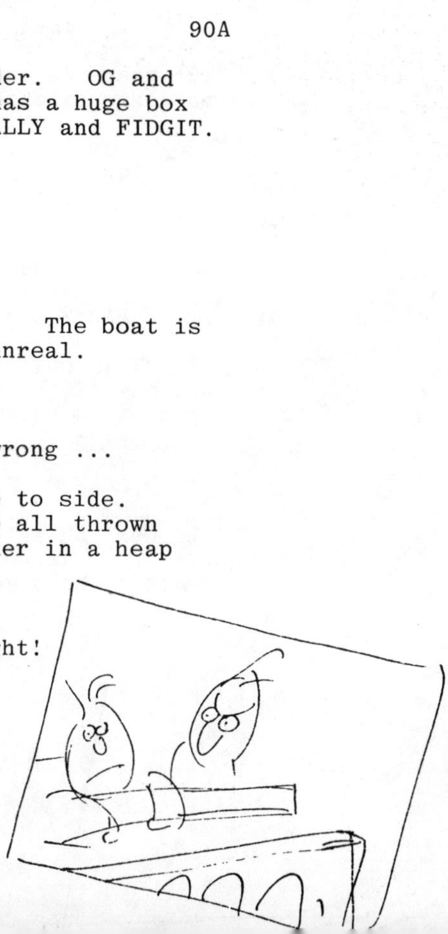

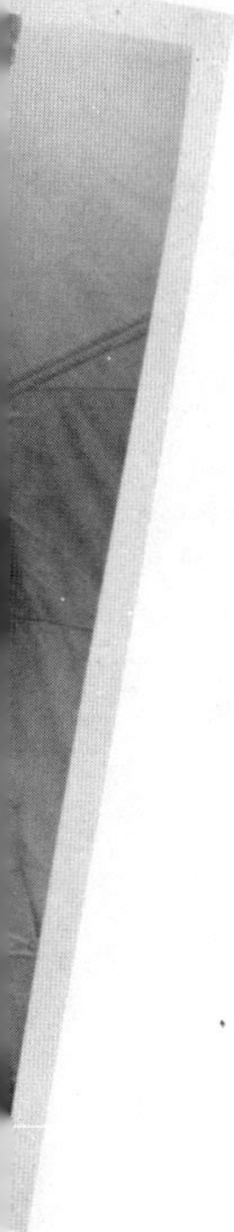

90A Continued 90A

At that moment, the boat lurches wildly to starboard and they are flung onto the other rail.

STRUTTER
I didn't do a thing, honestly ...

RANDALL
Drop the sail!!

WALLY grabs an axe and chops through the main line - the sail crashes down onto the deck. The boat is swaying around most unpredictably ...

RANDALL
All hands on the tiller!

All seven of the GANG clamber up to the bridge and grab hold of the tiller in an attempt to keep the vessel steady, but it still goes off course.

RANDALL
(desperately)
Hang on! Hang on! Keep her
steady!

The boat seems to respond and stops swaying.

That's better ... that's better ...

But there is a strange sound of rushing water, followed by an eerie silence.

WALLY
(the one nearest the
bows)
... er ... Randall ... Randall ...
I think there's something you
should know ...

91 EXT. MISTY SEA DAY 91

We CUT TO outside and see that the boat is actually rising up, out of the sea and into the sky ... It's resting on the head of an underwater GIANT ...

92 EXT. OGRE'S BOAT DAY 92

The DWARVES watch open-mouthed, as the deck sways ... They are swung around ... C.U. RANDALL's amazed look ... Quite suddenly he's galvanised into action. He gives the command.

Revised 6.5.80

92 Continued

RANDALL

Below decks!

PULL OUT to reveal that they've already gone. KEVIN is holding the door open ...

KEVIN

(beckons impatiently)

Come on!

93 EXT. MISTY SEA DAY 93

As the tiny figure of RANDALL slides down the pole, the GIANT's head glides swiftly through the sea.

94 INT. OGRE'S CABIN DAY

RANDALL rushes in to the huddled gang.

95 EXT. MISTY SEA DAY 95

The GIANT continues on his way unaware of the activity in the cabin. Somewhere in the distance is heard a baby's cry.

96 EXT. TROLL'S HOUSE DAY 96

CUT TO a tumbly down cottage at the edge of the sea. Outside sits an unhappy TROLL. From inside comes the fearsome cry of a BABY. Continually popping in and out of the door to rail at her husband and to scream at the BABY is a nagging TROLL WIFE. In the distance can be seen the GIANT's head making its way across the sea towards the TROLL's cottage. As they squabble in the foreground, the GIANT rises inexorably out of the sea, looming large and larger - his upper portions disappearing into the clouds. With each massive footstep the cottage shudders but the TROLLS, too immersed in their petty arguing, fail to notice. The GIANT, in turn, completely unaware of the existence of the TROLL family, manages to step directly on their house - just as MRS TROLL rushes inside to silence the BABY. With a mighty crunch and crash most of the house is flattened and both MRS TROLL and the BABY are silenced for good. The TROLL - without noticing the cause of the sudden peace and quiet - breathes a sigh of relief.

TROLL

Oomski! Zbbongg Khhuble!

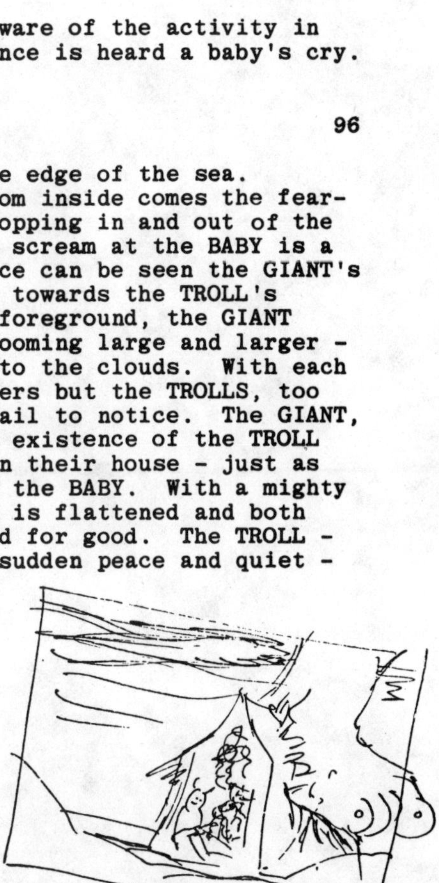

96A INT. OGRE'S CABIN DAY 96A

The GANG are desperate to find a way to stop the GIANT taking them too far off course. They start tearing up the floorboards of the cabin.

97 EXT GIANT'S HEAD DAY 97

As clouds swirl round his head, the GIANT continues on his way, but he becomes aware of a slight discomfort somewhere on top of his skull.

98 INT. OGRE'S CABIN DAY 98

The GANG have ripped up a section of the floor exposing part of the GIANT's bald head. OG has a sledge hammer and is hitting the GIANT's skull as hard as he can in a pathetic attempt to knock him out. The hammer bounces harmlessly off.

KEVIN, realising the futility of this, decides to do something stronger. He clambers up the steps to the OGRE's medicine chest and there, amongst all the remedies, finds a great jar of sleeping potion. Making his way to the kitchen, he grabs a bellows with a particularly long snout on it and fills it with the potion. Back at the GIANT's exposed pate, he squirts a bit of the potion into the air - like a doctor with a hypodermic needle of serum, and with a mighty jab injects the potion into the top of the GIANT's head.

99 EXT. GIANT'S HEAD DAY 99

The GIANT reacts to the injection as if he has just been bitten by a mosquito. He shifts the boat on his head.

100 INT. OGRE'S CABIN DAY 100

The GANG are thrown violently to one side as the boat shifts. Recovering, KEVIN peers out of a window.

101 EXT. GIANT'S HEAD DAY 101

The potion is taking effect. The GIANT is having difficulty keeping his eyes open.

102 EXT. MISTY WOOD DAY 102

The GIANT slumps. He pushes over a tree as he slowly settles down on the ground. He removes the ship from his head and dozes off.

103 INT. OGRE'S CABIN DAY 103

The GANG is toppled into a corner of the cabin as the boat comes to rest on its side. Slowly they regain their senses. Peering outside, they see the GIANT asleep. They scramble out of the cabin.

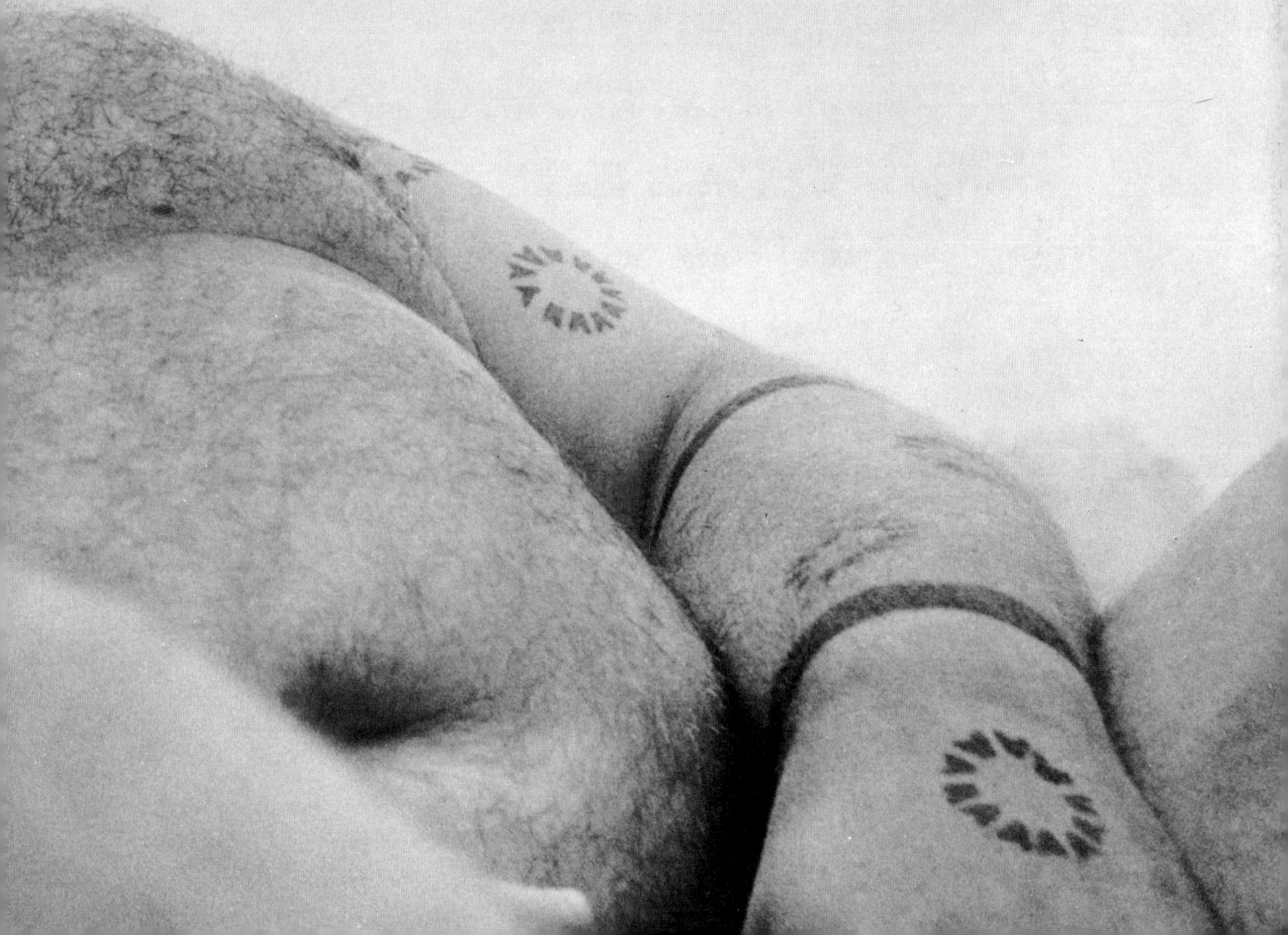

104 EXT. MISTY WOOD DAY 104

The GANG scramble off the boat. In the background the GIANT snores. They rush away.

105 EXT. MISTY PLACE DAY 105

The GANG runs off as fast as they can until they are completely obscured from sight in the swirling mist.

106 EXT. ROCKY LANDSCAPE DAY 106

The mist clears, revealing the GANG collapsed and lost and exhausted in a mysterious and eerie place. Strange rock forms loom up around them.

KEVIN
We're not getting anywhere, Randall, we're nowhere near the Most Fabulous Object in the World ...

RANDALL
(taking out the map)
We're not far away.

FIDGIT
Let's go back - before it's too late.

RANDALL looks up, then back, and shakes his head. He folds the map up ... PICTURE WOBBLE ...

107 INT. EVIL GENIUS' GROTTO DAY 107

BENSON
They are lost ... master ...

EVIL GENIUS
Let me see ... let me see, Benson ... Yes ...

The DWARVES are wandering about wearily trying to find a way out.

Yes .. but they are so near to me now .. that I can guide them to me.

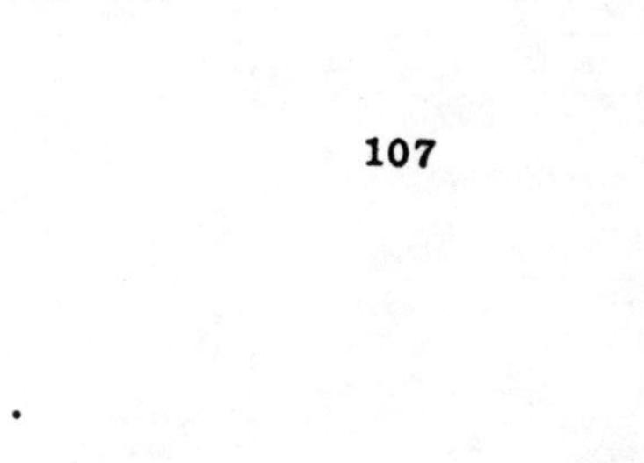

The PICTURE is SLOWLY CLOSING on OG.

... I must try to help them along the ... way.

108 EXT. ROCKY LANDSCAPE DAY

CLOSE ON OG looking very wide-eyed and scared.

108 EXT. ROCKY LANDSCAPE DAY 108

Suddenly, hiss, swish and whoosh! A moment that will make John Hurt's first encounter with the Alien look as fast as Churchill's funeral. OG cries out, he has been grabbed by the hairy sticky strands of a spidery web.

OG grunts fearfully as he is dragged rapidly OUT OF SHOT by some unseen force at the end of the web. The OTHERS race across and all hang on to him ... But they are dragged helplessly in a long line, holding on to each other's legs towards a strange cave mouth half-covered with a large spider's web.

109 INT. CAVE DAY 109

OG is dragged in to the dark interior of the cave. The thread pulling him turns out to be connected to knitting needles ominously clicking away in the hands of a desiccated OLD LADY. She has a COMPANION also knitting away silently. They are knitting great spider-like webs that completely fill the inside of the cave.

OLD KNITTER (MAISIE)
(hardly looking up)
Come in ...

2ND OLD KNITTER (MYRTLE)
(impatiently)
Come in, come in ...

They survey OG who's sprawled on the floor fighting out of the web.

MYRTLE
Oh dear ... oh dear ... oh dear ... what a disappointing catch, Maisie ... not my type at all.

Just then the rest of the DWARVES rush in.

MAISIE
Oh, they're not too bad.

MYRTLE
They're <u>awful</u>! Just as well we've got a few left ... What with winter coming on .

MAISIE
(looking at KEVIN)
What about that one ... he 's all right.

MYRTLE
(reprimanding MAISIE)
Don't be silly.

KEVIN struggles free and suddenly catches his breath in horror, as he looks into the gloom beyond the SPIDER LADIES ... CUT TO HIS POV.

109 Continued 109

Wrapped in the webs are several cocoon-shaped bundles, and in these bundles, bound tightly, their mouths gagged, are several young handsome blond KNIGHTS. Their eyes are filled with silent terror. The GANG begins to scramble back out of the door.

MYRTLE
(smiling at the mesmerised KEVIN)
So you're looking for the Most Fabulous Object in the World ...

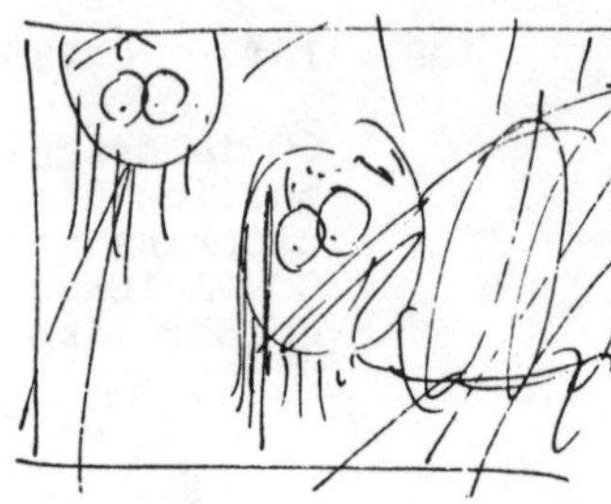

Ripple of surprise amongst the GANG.

RANDALL
How did you know ?

MYRTLE
That's why they all come past here.

MAISIE
Poor lost boys.

MYRTLE
We take them in and care for them, don't we Maisie ?

They laugh rather evilly together ... the eyes of the KNIGHTS look even more imploring ... MYRTLE crosses her legs revealing 2 more pairs of legs beneath her skirts. KEVIN's eyes bulge at this sight ... and then she crosses one of <u>these</u> pairs of legs.

MAISIE
Oh yes, Myrtle, they like it here ... they always want to stay ...

KEVIN's eyes meet the imploring, beseeching gaze of the KNIGHTS.

RANDALL
(interrupting the LADIES' private gigglings)
Is it far away ?

MYRTLE
What ?

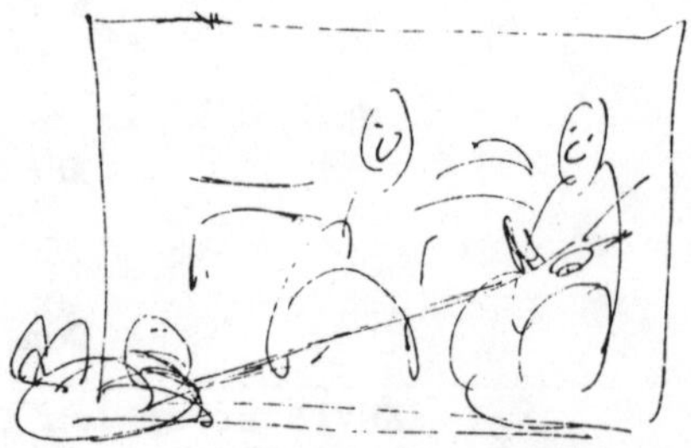

RANDALL
The Most Fabulous -

MYRTLE
Oh no .. not far away ....

KEVIN's hands grasp his Greek knife.

They go on knitting.

RANDALL
Can you tell us where ?

KEVIN lunges forward, knife up-raised, to try to free the KNIGHTS.

109 Continued 109

But he is caught, by the legs. He looks down. They're enmeshed in the spider web. He slashes at the web, and as he does so his arm and face is grabbed by another piece of webbing. He's trapped.

MYRTLE
(to MAISIE)
Now I don't think we can tell them if that's how they're going to behave ...

MAISIE
Certainly not!

KEVIN
(angrily, desperately)
You can't keep them here like that!

RANDALL
(rushing forward and restraining KEVIN)
(whispered)
Shut up!

KEVIN
I'm going to free them!

RANDALL
No you're not!

As he lunges forward, knife upraised, RANDALL quite neatly and sharply knocks him senseless with a karate chop to the neck. This impresses MAISIE greatly and stirs her somewhat to look on RANDALL with new eyes.

MAISIE
He's ... very manly ... couldn't we keep him ...

MYRTLE
(very definitely)
No.

RANDALL
(to MYRTLE)
Excuse me ... you were about to tell us how we find the Most Fabulous Object ...

109 Continued 109

MAISIE
(cutting him off)
(to RANDALL)
Do you want to stay and be our boyfriend ?

MYRTLE
(sharply)
Maisie ... pull yourself together ...

MAISIE
He's quite nice in a way.

MYRTLE
No he's not ... he's disgusting!

RANDALL
(agreeing quickly)
Yes that's right ... I'm very disgusting ...
now which way ... was ...

MAISIE
(with mounting excitement)
Can we have a party ?

MYRTLE
(to MAISIE)
Stop it!
(to RANDALL and GANG)
Go away you ... get out!

RANDALL
(backing towards the door)
Fine ... OK ... which way ... the Object ...

MYRTLE
(nastily, hurriedly)
Follow the pointing fingers.

MAISIE has got up and crossed to a rather old-fashioned cobwebby gramophone. She lifts the arm and settles it on a record.

RANDALL
The pointing fingers ?

MYRTLE
Yes ... now clear out.

MAISIE
It's party time ...

Very cool, intimate, jazzy party music, bluesy saxophone fills the little lair. As they hear it, the eyes of the LADIES' VICTIMS almost pop out in terror.

What a strange scene.

110 EXT. CAVE DAY 110

The GANG rush out of the cave dragging KEVIN. They scramble out of shot.

111 EXT. HAND FOREST EVENING 111

CUT TO gnarled root. The GANG stumble into shot and collapse.

KEVIN
(slowly coming round)
Where are we ?

RANDALL
I'm not sure exactly.

KEVIN
Did we save them ?

RANDALL
No, we saved you.

111 Continued 111

KEVIN starts to struggle angrily.

RANDALL
(pulling out map)
We've got to find the pointing fingers.

FIDGIT
(who has been looking
above them)
Uh...oh...

WALLY
(looking up)
I think we have.

CUT TO their P.O.V. Great hand/trees rise all around them, their fingers/branches reaching for the sky.

FIDGIT
Let's get out of here ... I don't
like it ...

RANDALL
(getting up)
No, we must be close now ... c'mon.

The GANG make their way through this strange forest of gigantic hand/trees. Horribly gnarled and twisted roots form the bases of these unpleasant growths. In the distance a WOOD CUTTER is chopping down a hand/tree. With each blow of the axe the hand writhes in agony. They pass several fallen hands clawing at the ground. This is a truly awful place. The GANG stop. Some of them start to shiver. Even VERMIN has lost some of his bounce.

111 Continued

FIDGIT
Let's go back ... now ...

RANDALL
We can't... we've got to go on.
Follow the pointing fingers

KEVIN
It's a trap

STRUTTER starts as a huge hand/tree comes crashing down near him. They are all in a highly nervous, almost hysterical state after their recent experiences.

STRUTTER
I'm not going any further... no-one knows what the hell we're supposed to be doing

OG
Yes! Yes! ... Yes!

OG has suddenly become very agitated. He is staring over their shoulders and pointing at something behind the group. They turn around. There, visible through the gap created by the felled tree, is a massive turreted citadel.

RANDALL
(grabs map - looks at it excitedly)
The Fortress of Ultimate Darkness!

OG
Yes, but that's not it.

RANDALL
What?

OG
(looking high into the sky)
Look!

The CAMERA PULLS BACK from the citadel to reveal that this massive structure is merely the gatehouse to an unbelievably immense building that stretches in every direction, farther than the eye can see. Slowly the CAMERA TILTS UP. Higher and higher the vast construction rises until it disappears into the clouds - a solid wall across the sky... well almost solid, for the massive facade is split by a gaping black crack that widens grotesquely as it reaches for the unseen heights. It is the most forbidding place imaginable. The GANG stands there awestruck. If a Fabulous Object Does Exist, then this surely is the place it would be found in. One by one even the most sceptical faces brighten with a mixture and the thrill of imminent wealth. Only KEVIN's face reflects deep disquiet. As they stand abreast the rise a cool wind licks at their clothing. A ripple.

111 Continued 111

RANDALL
(awesomely impressed)
We're there!

112 INT. EVIL'S GROTTO SUNSET 112

There is a great deal of activity.

112 Continued 112

EVIL

Now let them approach... poor pathetic wretches.

He laughs. His Henchmen laugh and applaud him.

113 EXT. HILL ABOVE THE CITADEL SUNSET 113

OG's eyes are shining. No-one wants to make the first move. KEVIN reacts with an anxious look around him, to the strange wind. The wind drops. OG leads off. With a last exchange of glances, making it clear that greed has won the day, the GANG descend the hill towards the citadel. In the background a hand/tree crashes to the ground. KEVIN heads off after the GANG.

114 EXT. CITADEL DAY 114

High up on the face of the citadel is a window from which S.R. Benson observes the approach of the GANG. As he looks down the CAMERA TILTS along the face of the gatehouse until it comes to rest on the DWARVES, far below, crossing the drawbridge.

115 EXT. CITADEL ENTRANCE DAY 115

The enormous portal engulfs the GANG as they hesitantly enter the citadel.

116 INT CITADEL SUNSET 116

The GANG creeps through the vast deserted entrance hall. Everything appears to be in a state of decay. There is no sign of life anywhere. This is a place of death. The floor is thick with dust undisturbed for centuries. As they make their way they leave behind a trail of footprints in the powdery floor covering. Cautiously, one of the DWARVES shouts hello. No answer. Just the echoing sounds of his own voice. The place is obviously deserted.

The light from the entrance leads them to a great pile of rubble in the centre of the hall. As VERMIN clambers up it he spots a skeletal arm sticking out of the debris. Ever hungry, he grabs it, but it seems to act as a switch - setting off a great rumbling and shaking. Dust and masonry fall from the heights. A column near the terrified GANG crashes down as a great jagged shaft of light races across the floor of the hall and up the wall. Looking in the direction of the light, the GANG see that it is pouring forth from a gigantic crack that has opened up in one of the walls. A siren song swells. The GANG rush towards the light, scrambling through the mammoth opening.

117 INT. FABULOUS HALL SUNSET 117

Coming out the other side of the crack the GANG stops awestruck. What they see is truly amazing - a dazzling apparition, the reflected aura of which at first just blinds our acquisitive little BAND. They look again straining and rubbing their eyes in the unaccustomed light and the image of something wonderful. And there beside it with teeth, suit, hair and eyes all gleaming with an unearthly radiance, is KEVIN's parents' favourite TV QUIZ SHOW COMPERE - manic grin frozen on his face. Music plays. The COMPERE's manic grin suddenly animates. His arm goes out to welcome them.

COMPERE

And here they are! The winners of the Most Fabulous Object in the World. The Answer to All Their Problems ... and yours .. is here! For them ... Tonight!

CUT TO wide shot of an infinitely huge black space broken by the occasional shaft of light. A gleaming pathway in the shape of a complex maze zigzags across this space - the sides of the pathway plummeting into unseeable depths from which the occasional wisp of smoke rises. On the far side of the maze the pathway ends in a square island platform rising above the abyss. Stairs ascend from the platform and at the top of them stands dazzling apparition - The Most Fabulous Object in the World. Too incandescent to be clearly made out, but obviously worth having. The COMPERE stands half-way up the stairs. Music crescendoes. The DWARVES are delighted but mesmerised.

DWARVES

Hey! Oh ... look! Hey! Us?

The AUDIENCE applause propels them forward.

KEVIN

No!

But it is too late to restrain the dazzled GANG. With cries of delight they rush forward to claim the thing they're told everybody wants. KEVIN is unable to restrain them.

As they rush desperately around the maze, the COMPERE is joined from behind by KEVIN's PARENTS, madly grinning and arrayed in glittering outfits. KEVIN is stunned. He doesn't know what to do. His parents urge him forward. He holds back. The DWARVES career madly through the maze. It's like a nightmare to KEVIN - the parents continue to beckon. The DWARVES have now reached the foot of the stairs and stop breathlessly. The COMPERE and KEVIN's PARENTS beam down at them. As the deliriously excited DWARVES make their final atavistic bid for ultimate greed, the blaze of golden light coalesces into ... A beautiful, shining, perspex and chrome, computerised, digitalised, de-ionised dream kitchen!

COMPERE (to the GANG)

Congratulations! But before you get the prize of a lifetime, can we have the map that brought you all this success!

He holds out his hands for the map, and RANDALL hands it over.

117 Continued 117

The Most Fabulous Object in the World suddenly disappears and in the place of the COMPERE and KEVIN's PARENTS stand EVIL, ROBERT and BENSON. The GANG Shriek and turn to run, but, with a deafening rumble and clang a sturdy iron cage descends around them trapping them inside. Helplessly they grab at the bars.

EVIL
I have the Map! I have the Map! And the day after tomorrow ..... the World!

He laughs a hideous triumphant cackling peal of demonic laughter.

118 INT. CAGE DAY 118

CUT TO rat crawling down heavy rope which supports the great metal cage in which KEVIN and the rest of the GANG sit disconsolately around - their legs dangling through the bars that make up the bottom of the cage. The cage is now hanging high above a bottomless black abyss. Some distance away are two similar cages in agonised poses. No-one speaks for a while. They are just alone with their failure.

118 Continued 118

Suddenly there is a loud squeak. VERMIN holds something. It wriggles.

VERMIN
Rat, anybody ?

No-one takes up the offer.

VERMIN
(muttering to himself)
Might be the last meal we'll get...

He disconsolately opens his mouth, but we CUT TO STRUTTER before anything really revolting can happen. STRUTTER stares at the floor.

STRUTTER
Well....that's it, then...

WALLY
It's all over.

FIDGIT
...How could we have been so stupid ?

OG
(thoughtfully)
I dunno....

A pause.

CUT TO a photo of Greece. Some idyllic scene taken by KEVIN's Polaroid. He's looking at it with tears in his eyes...KEVIN sorts through two more Polaroids. Pictures of Mycenae and AGAMEMNON which bring back intolerable memories for him. Then at the bottom of the pile he comes across a photo of the DWARVES in better times, flaunting their wares in Sherwood Forest. He passes it over and onto another Greek scene. A pause. Then he quickly goes back to the group photo. He stares at it, then he rummages hurriedly in his bag and produces a magnifying glass. He applies it to the photo, looking, not at the faces but focussing...on the map that they are proudly holding up. He peers more closely. Yes, the details are visible.

KEVIN
Hey!

All the DWARVES turn. They'd almost forgotten him. KEVIN clambers to his feet, and across to the DWARVES.

KEVIN
Look at this!

118 Continued 118

They gather round the photo, he holds the magnifying glass.

FIDGIT
Good one of Wally ...

KEVIN (excitedly)
No look ...

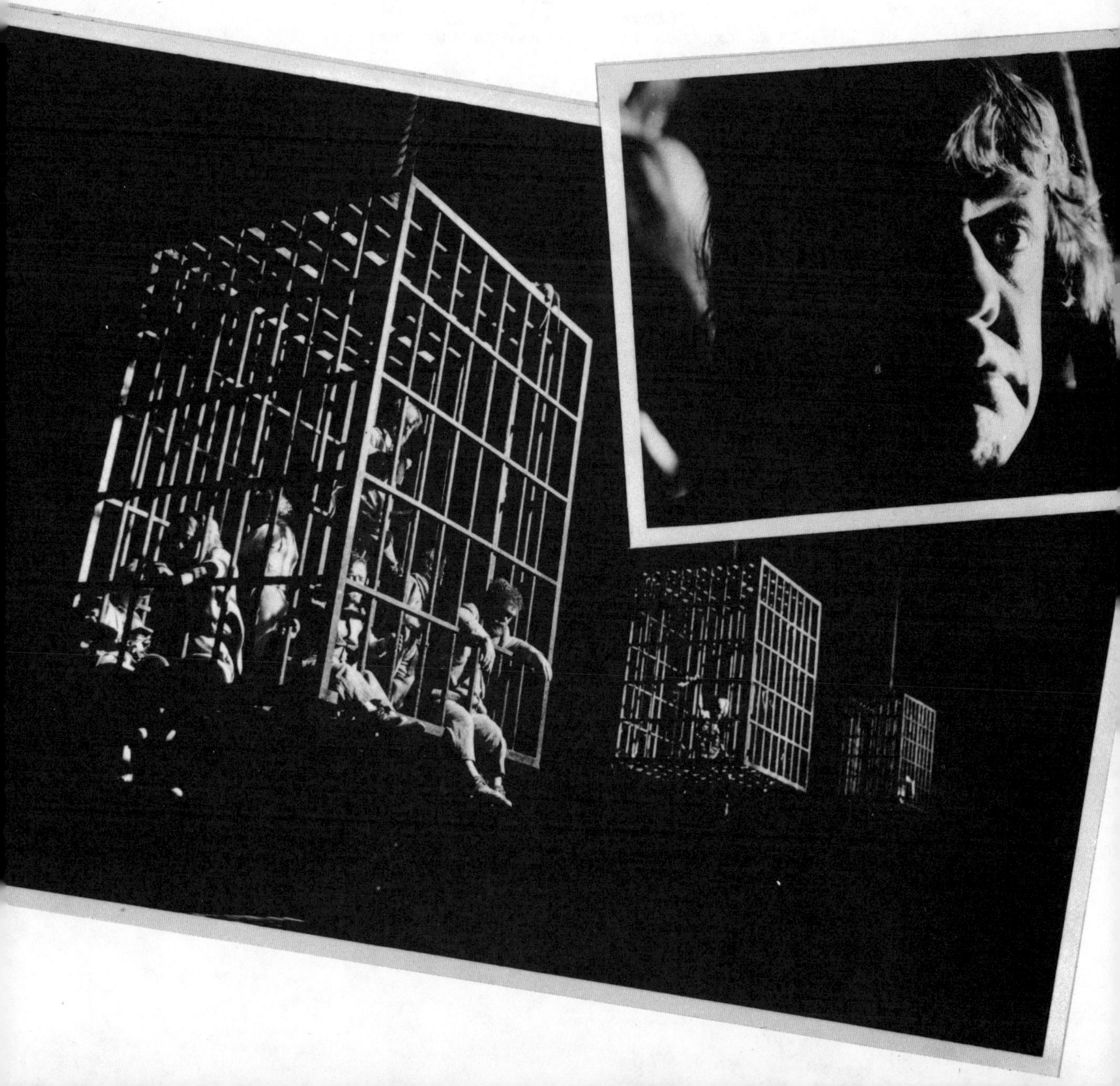

118 Continued 118

They look closer.

KEVIN
D'you see what I see ?

Grunts of incomprehension from the disillusioned band.

KEVIN
The map!

RANDALL
(impatiently)
We can see it's the map .. but what use
is it to us now ...

KEVIN
Look closer ...
the Time of Legends .. see .. ?
See the Fortress of Ultimate Darkness ?

RANDALL
Yes ...

KEVIN
Well, look .. right below it ..

Suddenly RANDALL lets out a low whistle of amazement.

RANDALL
That's a hole ?

KEVIN
Well, look....

RANDALL
But look at the size of it!

KEVIN
Exactly!

RANDALL
It must lead anywhere ...

KEVIN
Everywhere ...

STRUTTER
What ?

RANDALL
Look ... we've just found the biggest
hole in the Universe and it's practically
right underneath our feet.
(getting up)
Kevin ... you're a genius ... Come
on you lot ... shift ...

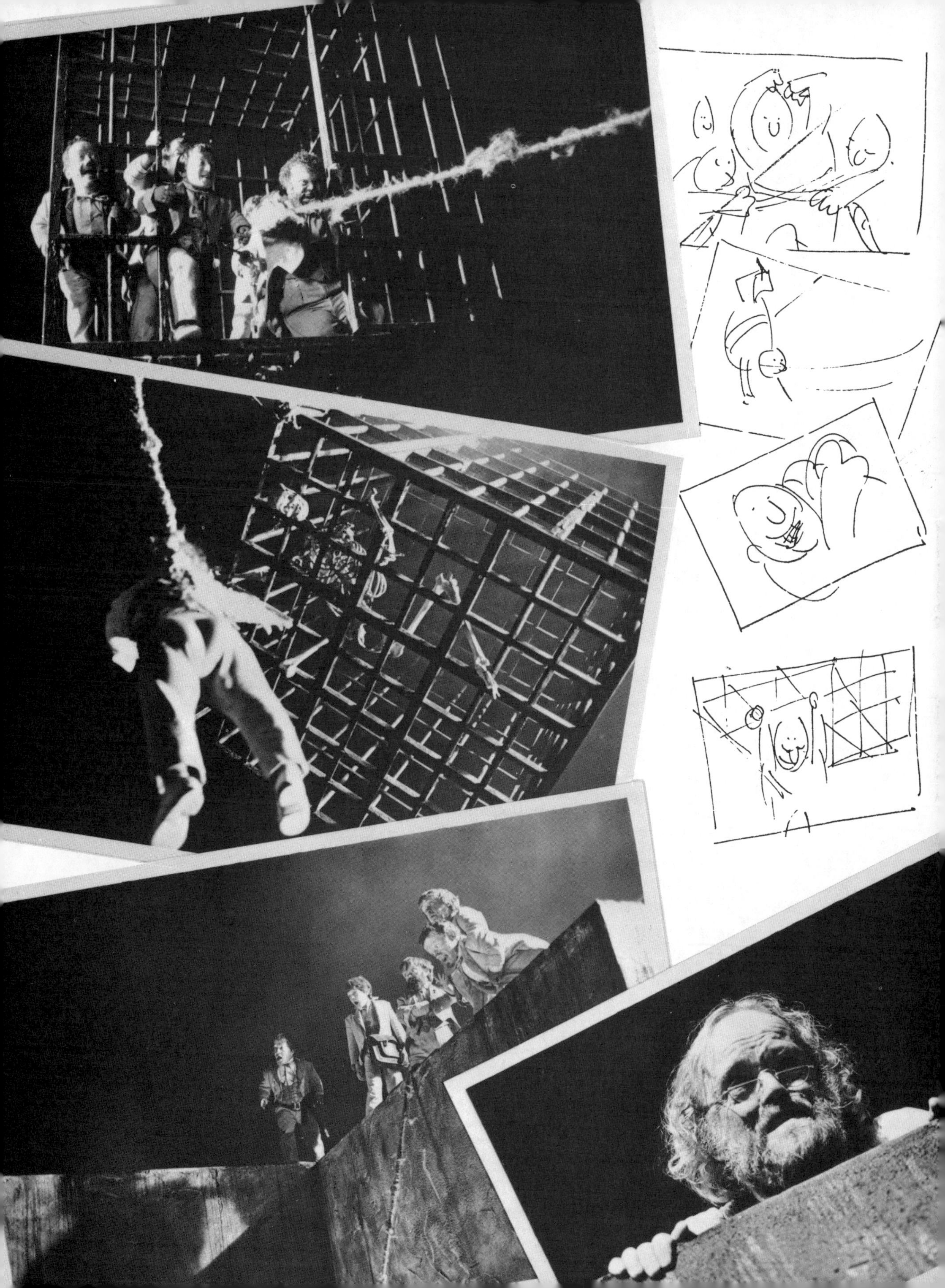

118 Continued 118

FIDGIT
(in alarm)
We'll never get out of here!

OG
(springing into action)
Want a bet?

RANDALL
That's it Og ... we'll show 'em we can do <u>something</u> right ....

They work well and go into action methodically... OG is already studying the lock ... he grabs KEVIN's bag and rummages through. OG's eyes light up. He roots out the knife the Greek King gave him. KEVIN tries to stop him, but realising it's for the cause, he reluctantly lets OG take it.

OG slips it into the lock, and with much bending and twisting, which from KEVIN's reactions we see is giving him heart-failure ... the door swings open.

OG hands KEVIN his knife back with a grin of thanks. The end of the beautiful Greek blade is now twisted into a perfect corkscrew.

RANDALL snatches the knife out of KEVIN's hands and hands it to FIDGIT who scrambles up the outside of the now swinging cage. With the knife he begins to cut off strands from the supporting hauser. He drops them down to WALLY and STRUTTER who start to braid them. Sometime later they have woven a long thin rope. The hauser holding the cage is extremely frayed. The GANG is working against time - with each movement of the cage another of the few remaining strands of the hauser snaps. Tying the rope around STRUTTER's waist they lower him down below the cage. Slowly they begin to swing him back and forth. With each swing he arcs further out. The hauser continues to part with these exertions. At last STRUTTER has gained enough momentum and with a final swing he reaches the neighbouring cage. He clings to the bars as WALLY is tied to the rope. Pulling it taut and checking his angle of attack, WALLY leaps from the cage. Gracefully he arcs under STRUTTER's cage and sweeps over to the next cage. The moment he has firmly grasped its bars, STRUTTER lets go and swings under WALLY and onto solid ground at the edge of the abyss. A cheer goes up from the rest of the GANG.
STRUTTER attaches the rope to a stone column. The other end is attached to the cage, and after WALLY has untied himself from the middle of it, the rope is pulled taut.
One by one, the GANG slides down the rope to the ground.
WALLY checks his positioning and fearlessly lets go of the cage and drops towards the rope. Expertly he catches it but the jolt on the rope snaps the hauser holding the cage, and the cage and rope plummet into the abyss. WALLY disappears as well. Panic from the GANG. MADLY they pull on the rope. Up it comes ... and, surprise, WALLY is dangling on the end. Relief all round.

118 Continued 118

RANDALL wipes his brow, his eyes shine with relief and triumph.

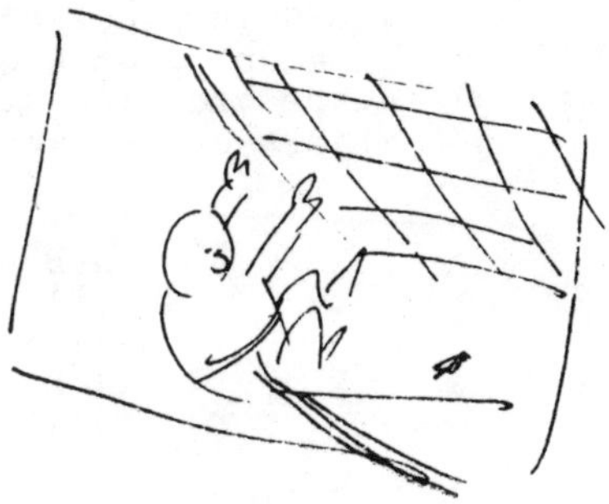

RANDALL
We've done it!

KEVIN
Now all we need is the map ...

RANDALL
What ?

KEVIN
We must get the map.

RANDALL
Don't be a fool, we know where the hole is, let's get out of here ...

He makes to go, KEVIN grabs him.

KEVIN
Evil's got the map ... Randall!

RANDALL
Damn right .. the last thing we want to do is see him again ... come on, quick!

He makes to go, but KEVIN holds him firmly back.

KEVIN
We can't leave him with the map, Randall - he'll destroy the world!

CUT TO SCENE 120.

PAGE 109/SCENE 119 DELETED

120 INT. EVIL'S GROTTO DAY 120

EVIL and his two slavering ASSISTANTS are poring over the map. Around them are scattered various evil appurtenances, including skeletons, skulls and little black aprons. EVIL is moaning with quiet pleasure ... his most personable lump - the drooling attendant BENSON, is beside him ...BENSON thinks and speaks, and indeed exists, with difficulty.

EVIL
Oh Benson ... I feel the power of evil coursing through my veins, filling every corner of my being with the desire to do wrong ... I feel so bad, Benson ...

BENSON
Good ... good ...

EVIL

Yes, it is good ... for this is the worst sort of badness I am feeling ..

BENSON
Kill me! Kill me! Master ..

EVIL
Not yet Benson. We have work to do ... no less a work than to overthrow creation itself. We will remake man in our image, not his, we will turn the mountains into sea ..

121 INT. ENTRANCE TO EVIL'S GROTTO DAY 121

The GANG arrive outside the door. KEVIN peers through the keyhole.

RANDALL
This is madness

EVIL
(continued from inside)
.. and we will make the sea into fire and the fire into a mighty rushing wind that will cover the face of the earth and wipe clean the scourge of woolly thinking once and for all ...

RANDALL
(pushing KEVIN aside)
Here, let me see.
(peers through keyhole)

122 INT. EVIL'S GROTTO DAY 122

BENSON
(trying, with considerable effort, to equal his master's passionate sense of mission)
we can make....beans into peas...

EVIL
Oh Benson, dear Benson....you are so mercifully free of the ravages of intelligence.

BENSON
You say such nice things, master...

EVIL
Yes....I'm sorry....now Benson... I'm going to have to turn you into a dog for a while.

BENSON
Thank you master....

There is a flash.

123 INT ENTRANCE TO EVIL'S GROTTO DAY 123

The GANG reels back.

124 INT EVIL'S GROTTO DAY 124

Sure enough, a black drooling MONGREL now sits on the table with the map, where BENSON used to be.

EVIL
Guard the map, Benson.

DOG barks in acquiescence

EVIL turns to the pool through which he has watched the outside world.

EVIL
Robert, we must plan a New World together...
(ROBERT grunts)
...but this time we will start properly. Tell me about computers.

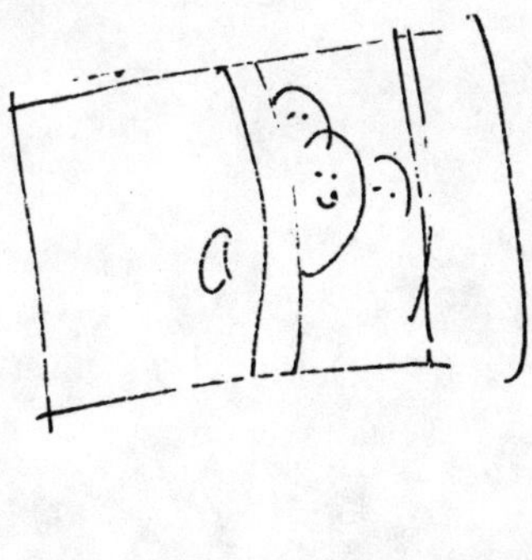

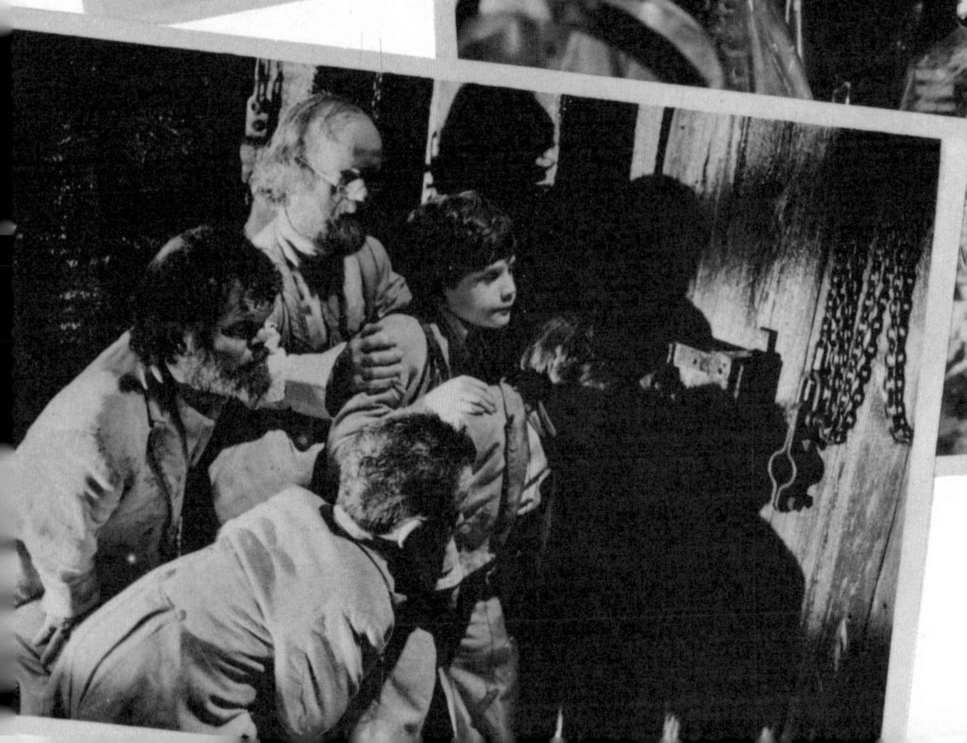

124 Continued

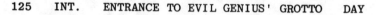

ROBERT
(a lurking hulk, who is almost as limited as BENSON in his grasp of the basic essentials of language)
A computer is an automatic electronic apparatus for making calculations or controlling operations that are expressible in numerical or logical terms.

125 INT. ENTRANCE TO EVIL GENIUS' GROTTO DAY 125

Outside the door KEVIN beckons the others to enter. They slowly push the door open.

126 INT. EVIL GENIUS' GROTTO DAY

EVIL is getting frighteningly excited.

EVIL
And fast breeder reactors ?

ROBERT
Fast breeder reactors use a fast fission process for the generation of fissile isotopes ...

The GANG tiptoes in. The DOG barks. They freeze and back into the shadow.

EVIL turns.

EVIL
Quiet Benson! ... Show me more, Robert ... show me more ... show me subscriber trunk dialling. I must know everything.

The DWARVES move forward, again the DOG barks. KEVIN stops, almost beside a skeleton. Suddenly he has an idea, Stealthily he reaches for a skeleton's leg ... picks it up and flings it into a corner of the room. BENSON the DOG runs after it.

OG and VERMIN race forward to the table. OG leaps on VERMIN's shoulders, grabs the map (which is rolled up, like a scroll). He tosses it to RANDALL, who catches it and throws it to KEVIN.

KEVIN
(hisses)
Quick!

126 Continued 126

He holds the door as they turn and race out. The scuffling makes EVIL whip round from his screen ... he registers the map has gone ... and screams:

EVIL
Stop!

126 Continued 126

But they are all out of the door and safely away, except for OG who slips as he makes for the door. The EVIL GENIUS, eyes blazing, fires his fingertip rockets by bending back his mandarin fingernails in rapid succession. OG bursts into a blaze of tiny explosions.

127 INT. ENTRANCE TO EVIL'S GROTTO DAY 127

The flash of light from inside illuminates VERMIN as he hurls himself out of the door and joins the others. A second later OG emerges. He is, however, only OG from the waist downwards. Above that he has been changed into a pig.

Quick reactions of OTHERS looking horrified... but there's no time to be lost. From inside we hear a shriek of malevolent anger ....

128 INT. BRIDGE TO EVIL'S GROTTO DAY 128

EVIL
After them! Stop them by every means in my power!

From the mouth of the gargoyle entrance a gigantic fireball vomits forth ... just as the GANG clear the bridge.

129 INT. CITADEL CORRIDORS DAY 129

The GANG rush back the way they came. Behind them the sound of distant footsteps thunders through the halls. The GANG races on. Wind begins to howl around them. Strange swirling lighting begins to illuminate the place. Suddenly, in front of them, the stone flooring begins to burst apart. From under the floor rises a horrific GHOUL. Another section of the floor bursts open. Another GHOUL appears. "Terrifying!" T. Gilliam
The GANG detours. With these howling apparitions blocking their way to the dungeon KEVIN decides they must separate.

RANDALL
What..?

KEVIN
(showing map)
This is what he wants ... I'll draw them away ...

129 Continued 129

FIDGIT
What about us?

KEVIN
You go and get help down the hole, go wherever you can and bring back whatever you can find.

WALLY
You can't stay on your own.

KEVIN
I'll take one other...

(OG grunts enthusiastically)

KEVIN
Alright Og ... let's give them something to chase ... Good luck to the rest of you!

130 INT. CITADEL CORRIDORS DAY 130

KEVIN and OG dodge through the corridors. Fireballs whirl past them. Baying sinister SHAPES crash after them. The evil forces get closer and closer.

131/132 DELETED 131/132

133 INT. GREAT HALL DAY 133

KEVIN and OG charge through a doorway and discover themselves in a colossal hall. The floor and one sloping stone wall are coloured in a gigantic chequerboard pattern. Great stone blocks are piled up in odd formations. A large section of the ceiling has collapsed and light streams in from this jagged opening high above. In the centre of this pool of light stands EVIL. Behind the BOY and the DEMI-PIG are EVIL's FORCES. They are trapped. EVIL gazes smugly at KEVIN.

EVIL
You are a very troublesome little fellow I think I should teach you one of my special lessons....
(BENSON sniggers ingratiatingly at his side)
What do you think, Benson? What would look nice? Half donkey, half warthog, ... half oyster, half goat ... or perhaps the diseased left tonsil of a geriatric alligator!

More knowing laughter. EVIL suddenly stops grinning. He looks hard and terrifying and straight into KEVIN's eyes.

133 Continued 133

KEVIN grabs a torch from a nearby column and holds the map beside it. EVIL snarls ....KEVIN has the initiative again.

KEVIN
Call off those ... creatures ... or
I destroy the map for ever ..

EVIL
Don't be so ..

KEVIN
Call them off!

EVIL
Very well! I have no need of them.
Benson, your time has come.

BENSON
Oh wonderful, wonderful, Master!

EVIL turns to the dog BENSON, raises his hands, a cracking flash of light encircles BENSON and he falls with a scream from sight in the black depths of the abyss. He explodes with a mighty roar, and then another, and another. Bits fly high into the air bursting into more and more elaborate displays of pyrotechnics. Roman candles shriek. Spluttering bits of material bounce near the cage and then shoot off into the air to burst into amazing showers of flame. Finally with a final glorious starburst that sends bits of phosphoresence raining down on the hall, BENSON is no more.

EVIL
But I am a reasonable man. Give me
the map and you may at least walk out
of here ... on human feet.

KEVIN
No!

EVIL puts his hand out. A shaft of light flashes and curls onto OG. OG turns into a total pig. KEVIN looks horrorstruck ... d'you hear ? - horrorstruck ... EVIL is advancing, hand outstretched ...

KEVIN
No! ... No!

EVIL is close, quick as a flash his arm goes up. KEVIN screams and clutches his face; when he looks he sees EVIL leering in triumph, map held aloft, and about to do something very nasty to KEVIN. He advances, KEVIN hurls himself to the floor. EVIL turns and is about to crush him when suddenly there is an almighty crash. KEVIN thinks he's dead and instinctively shuts his eyes tight. But when he opens them he sees the EVIL GENIUS has frozen with arm upraised and is staring behind KEVIN. Nothing

LZY

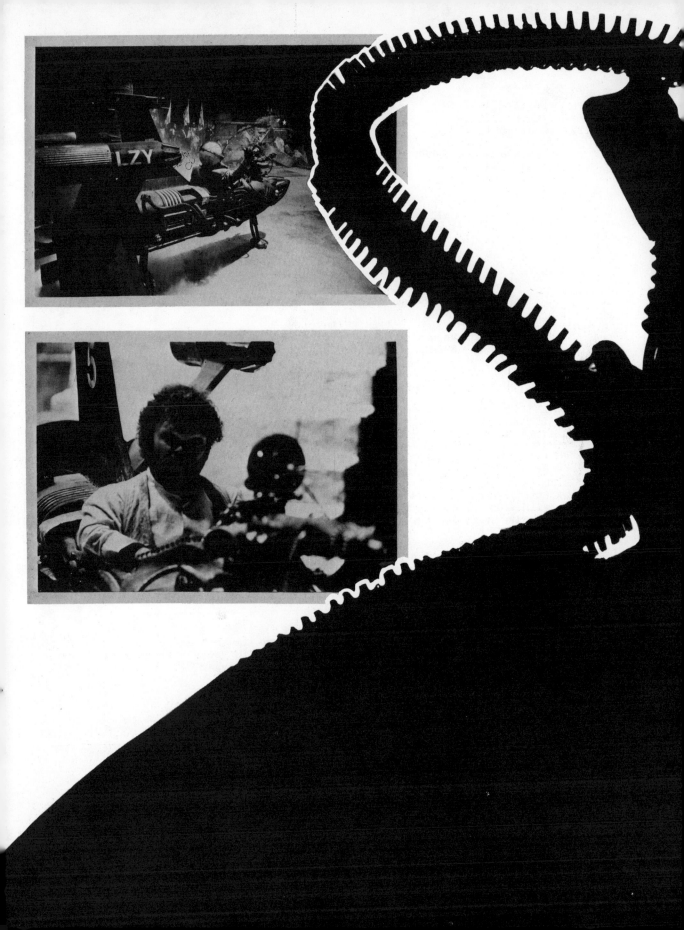

133 Continued 133

less than a huge Sherman tank bursts its way through the wall with RANDALL at the controls.

KEVIN is amazed. From another doorway a cry of "Kevin!" and a group of mounted fully-armoured KNIGHTS led by STRUTTER gallop up to KEVIN's side. A strange whining noise announces the arrival of a futuristic laser gun device. Descending on anti-gravity pads from above their heads, WALLY is manoeuvring it into position. From somewhere else in the dark recesses of the hall comes gunfire and a POSSE of American COWBOYS gallops up, whooping and hollering as they do. VERMIN rides with one of them. KEVIN whirls round unable to take it all in. Finally to the clatter of a horse-drawn chariot, FIDGIT arrives. He stands in the chariot. Behind him at a dog-trot are a company of GREEK ARCHERS.

EVIL looks around the assembled FORCES with an amused and disdainful smile.

EVIL
So this is the best that the Supreme Being can do?

CHIEF COWBOY
Is that the bohunk who's causing all the trouble? Well we won't have no problem there ... come on guys ... we'll have this dude for breakfast...

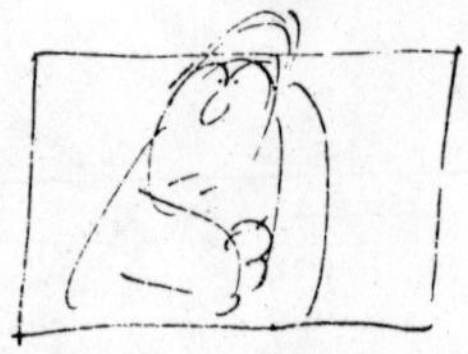

COWBOYS
Yessir!

Before KEVIN can stop them they charge off towards EVIL. Lassoos whirling they bear down on him with mighty whoops and hollers. Great fun this. A lariat snakes out and lassoos EVIL with ease. Another encircles him. And then another. The EVIL GENIUS does nothing. The COWBOYS tighten the slack on the ropes. They surround him. He can't move.

COWBOY LEADER
(shouts back to Kevin)
See, no problem, sonny. You can call your men off! We'll bring him in - aaaaarghh!

At that very moment he is whipped off his horse. So are the other COWBOYS. EVIL has begun to spin. Faster and

133 Continued 133

faster he spins. The COWBOYS hold on for dear life at the end of their ropes. Higher and higher they spin. Faster and faster whirls EVIL. The GANG looks on in horror. From the centre of the red whirling SHAPE that is EVIL comes an arm with a vicious-looking knife. It hesitates for a moment, and then, slices. The ropes part and the COWBOYS sail through the air... right through the window opening high in the wall. One of them arcs right over the heads of KEVIN's FORCES and is gone. The COWBOYS are all dead. EVIL has stopped spinning and laughs. The GANG is stunned into silence. KEVIN is angry.

He summons the KNIGHTS and deploys them in a great semi-circle around EVIL. At the BOY's signal they charge. Their mighty horses shake the ground with their pounding hooves. Deadly lances point directly at EVIL as the KNIGHTS cannon towards him. Calmly he removes from the folds of his robe a gas mask. Securing it in place he throws his arms upwards. From the sleeves of his costume great jets of thick black smoke shoot skywards. The KNIGHTS are practically upon him when a curtain of black smoke descends around them. Obscured from view, the KNIGHTS can be heard to be wreaking the most awful vengeance on the unfortunate EVIL GENIUS. The BOY and the DWARVES wait expectantly. Suddenly all is quiet. And then, from the depths of the black smoke appears a horse - galloping riderless away. A second horse appears. Also riderless. Then another. And another. The BOY and the DWARVES stand aghast as the smoke lifts revealing a tangled mass of KNIGHTS - all impaled on each other's lances. They form a terrible free-standing sculpture. EVIL stands next to his work smiling smugly.

VERMIN orders his ARCHERS forward. They rush into position and, drawing back their bows, let fly a deadly shower of arrows. As the arrows course across the sky EVIL swirls his red robe around him with a defiant sweep. Pulling back, we can see he has turned himself into a giant red pincushion - complete with giant thimble, needle and thread. The arrows thump into the soft pincushion. Drawing in a huge breath, EVIL expands the pincushion. And then, with a great grunt, he expels the arrows from the pincushion - sending them flying back to where they came from. Everyone runs for cover but to no avail. The ARCHERS are wiped out to the last man. KEVIN orders the tank and the laser gun to open up on EVIL but EVIL is able to control the machines. The DWARVES can't stop them from being turned on KEVIN and the others. The machines have gone berserk. The GANG is caught in the crossfire. The tank rumbles towards them. KEVIN slips and is about to be crushed under the tracks when FIDGIT races out to save him. In so doing, FIDGIT himself is hurled beneath a huge column of rock. EVIL deflects the fire from WALLY's laser rockets at the rock which crashes down burying FIDGIT.

133 Continued 133

KEVIN looks back at the smoking pile of rubble. His eyes fill with tears that pour uncontrollably down his cheeks. Through it all his anger returns. Defiantly he confronts the snarling figure of EVIL triumphant. The GANG cowers in absolute terror. There is nowhere else to run. All except WALLY who rushes to FIDGIT's body .. He can't believe what EVIL has done. WALLY advances on the laughing, smiling EVIL. WALLY shouts, screams, calls him a murderer, a scum ... The others try to restrain him. The figure of EVIL seems to swell, the leer becomes terrifyingly ugly. The eyes burn down. He begins to glow as he summons all his terrifying power. The DWARVES look helplessly for cover but all is destroyed. The GANG screams.

Then suddenly, from somewhere behind them a gigantic bolt of lightning splits the air and strikes EVIL dead centre. He turns to carbon. A perfect charcoal replica of his former self - petrified for ever. KEVIN and the DWARVES spin around to see who or what it was that saved them. Lo and behold, it is none other than the SUPREME BEING. The DWARVES are at once elated and at the same time terrified. The SUPREME BEING has finally caught up with them.

RANDALL
(prostrating himself
on the floor and urging
the others to do the same)
Get down! Get down!

Then, the SUPREME BEING suddenly, before their very averted eyes, metamorphoses from his glowing radiant impressive long white-flowing bearded self to a rather ordinary bureaucrat in a not very well-fitting suit.

He shakes himself. He seems to be tired and irritable. He's not unlike Alec Guiness playing George Smiley, but quite unlike Dirk Bogarde in "The Spanish Gardener".

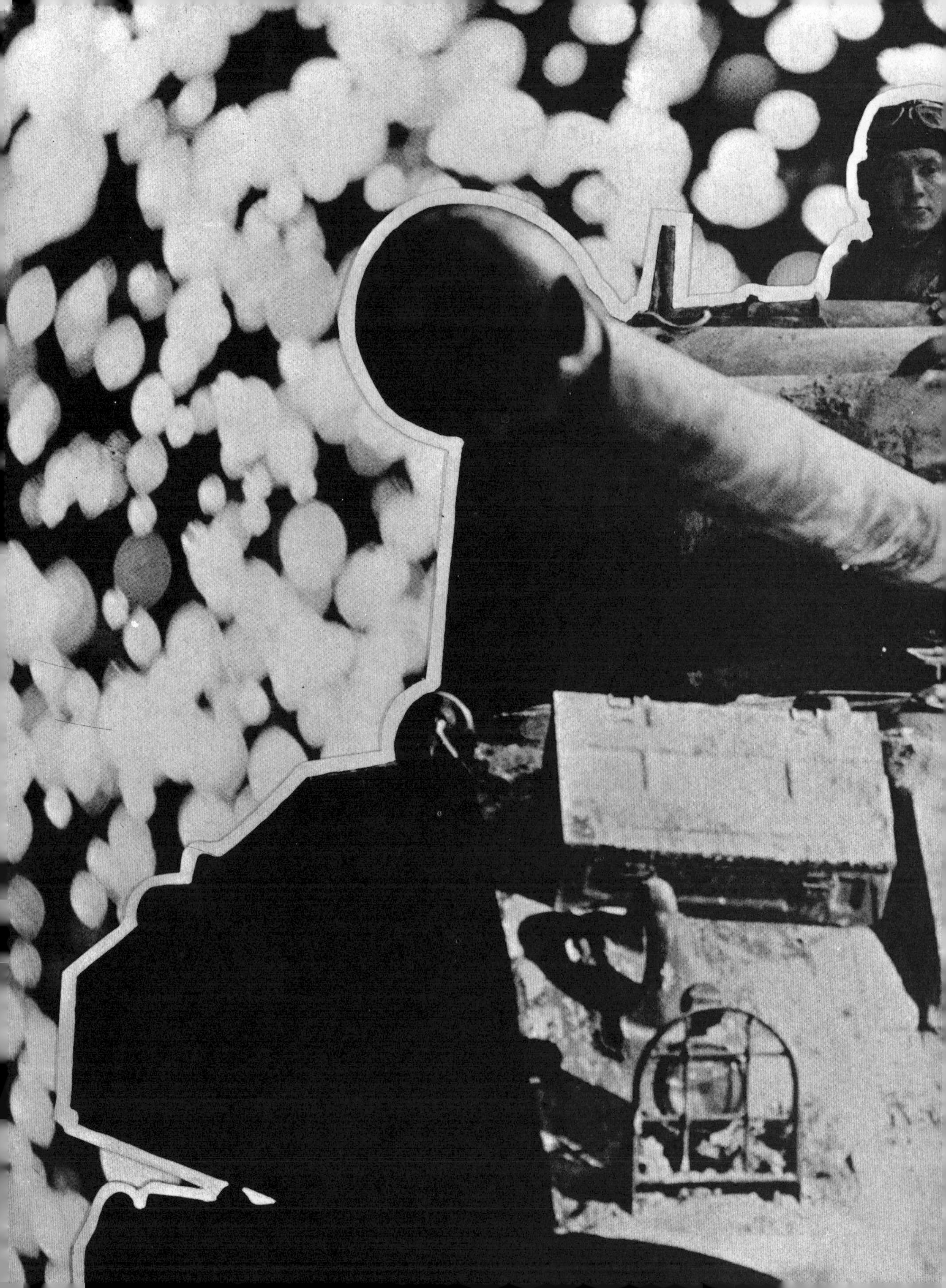

133 Continued 133

SUPREME BEING (with distaste)
Oh ... I hate having to appear like that. It really is the most tiresome noisy manifestation. Still - rather expected of one I am afraid.

RANDALL
(beckoning to the others to prostrate themselves)
Get down ... get down ...

But RANDALL is on his knees.

RANDALL
Oh Great One, Supreme Being ... Creator of the Universe, without Whom we would be mere scarab beetles on the dung heap of humanity ...

SUPREME BEING
Is the pig with you?

The GANG nods.

Right, better sort him out first.

He looks briefly in OG's direction. OG changes before their very eyes from pig to OG.

OG
(sadly)
Oh, I was enjoying that.

SUPREME BEING
(fussily)
If there's one thing I can't stand, it's mess ... Come on, pick all this stuff up ...

RANDALL
Oh yes sir ... of course sir ...
(he scrambles to his feet and starts to clear up)
(hissing to WALLY who is crouched over the body of FIDGIT)
Wally, come on, come and help.

WALLY
(with tears streaming down his trousers)
He's dead, Randall, Fidgit's dead.

133 Continued 133

SUPREME BEING
Oh is that all. Well, he doesn't get
out of work that easily.

He gestures and the collapsed column rises and FIDGIT gets up.

WALLY
Fidgit!

FIDGIT
(slightly confused)
Wally ? What is it ?

WALLY
(hugging FIDGIT)
Fidgit, I killed you!

FIDGIT
Well, you didn't do it very well.

SUPREME BEING
(impatiently)
Oh hurry up!

RANDALL
Oh sir ... oh Great One ... we can
explain everything honestly we didn't
mean to steal the map ... we didn't mean
to run away ... we
(he recovers map from debris)

SUPREME BEING
What do you mean, you didn't mean to
steal the map ?

RANDALL
(haplessly, dusting map off)
Well it just sort of ...

SUPREME BEING
(grabbing map from RANDALL)
Of course you didn't mean to steal the
map .... I gave it to you ... you silly man ..
and this
(indicating a particular bit
of filth on the floor - RANDALL
rushes to pick it up - the
others are all cleaning)
D'you really think I didn't know ?

RANDALL's mouth falls open.

RANDALL
Mmm?

133 Continued 133

SUPREME BEING
I had to have some way of testing my handiwork ... I think Evil turned out rather well, don't you?

RANDALL
What sir?

SUPREME BEING
Evil! Turned out rather well - mmm? Whose are these ?
(he holds out KEVIN's original clothes)

KEVIN
Mine, sir.

SUPREME BEING
You really are an untidy boy ...
(he hands them over, then holds out pad and pen)
Sign here.

KEVIN signs. SUPREME BEING checks signature and puts book away. Meanwhile the truth is slowly dawning ....

WALLY
You mean you knew what was happening to us ?

SUPREME BEING
Well, of course ... I am the Supreme Being ...I'm not entirely dim.

RANDALL
No sir, no sir .... of course ... it's just that we ...

SUPREME BEING
I let you take the map ... I chased you as slowly as I convincingly could .... quite honestly there were times when I nearly gave up the whole test.... Now I want every bit of Evil placed in here ... right away ...

He indicates a huge letter-box. The DWARVES set to picking up the charcoal figure of EVIL.

ALL
Oh yes sir .... right away sir...

KEVIN
You mean, you let all those people die just to test your creation ?

133 Continued 133

SUPREME BEING
Yes ... you're rather a clever little chap ... I was rather pleased with the way I made you ...

KEVIN
But why did they have to die ?

SUPREME BEING
You might as well say why do we have to have Evil ...

RANDALL (quickly)
Oh we wouldn't dream of asking that ...

KEVIN
Yes, why do we have to have Evil ?

SUPREME BEING
Ah.... I think it's something to do with free will ... Oh be careful!

The GANG in their haste have dropped the figure of EVIL. It breaks into several pieces. One piece rolls behind a bit of debris .. unnoticed by the GANG.

SUPREME BEING
That's concentrated Evil ... one drop of that could turn you all into hermit crabs ..

RANDALL
Sorry sir! Sorry ... so ... I um ... do you think we might have our jobs back then ?

SUPREME BEING
Well ... you certainly were appallingly bad robbers ... I should really do something frightfully extrovert and vengeful with you .. but I'm honestly too tired .. so I think I'll just transfer you to the Undergrowth Department ... bracken, small shrubs, that sort of thing - with a 19% cut in salary backdated to the beginning of time ...

They all nod gratefully.

GANG
(touching forelocks)
Thank you ... thank you ...

SUPREME BEING
(drily)
Yes, well I am the nice one.

133 Continued 133

SUPREME BEING
(indicating the container full of EVIL)
Is it all there ?
(GANG nod - but they still haven't spotted the missing bit)
Right ... come on then ... back to Creation. I mustn't waste any more time ... Everyone'll think I've lost control again ... put it down to evolution...

FIDGIT
Sir...?

SUPREME BEING
(testily)
Yes ...

FIDGIT
(Indicating KEVIN)
What about my friend, sir ... can he come with us?

SUPREME BEING
This isn't a school outing....

FIDGIT
But sir ... he deserves something ... without him ...

SUPREME BEING
Oh don't go on about it ... he's got to stay here, to carry on the fight ... come on all of you!

And with that he transmogrifies ... at the moment of transmogrification a voice booms out of the light ...

Oh I do hate this sort of thing.

KEVIN
Hey ... please don't leave me .... please.

Rushing wind noise, and a blinding light suffuses the battle-wrecked hall.

GANG
(slightly worried and rushed)
Bye Kevin ... bye Kevin ... good luck ...

KEVIN
Don't leave me .. don't leave me.

Smoke from the piece of EVIL GENIUS begins to rise up and swirl around him. He notices it and starts to scream while coughing and choking.

133 Continued 133

KEVIN
Please don't leave me!

132 INT. KEVIN'S BEDROOM DAWN 134

KEVIN wakes up in his bed ... smoke is all around him.

KEVIN
(half-asleep)
Don't leave me ... please ...

Smoke is billowing into the room .. and the door is being bashed down. FIREMEN rush in.

FIREMAN
Come on ... come on ...

KEVIN
What happened ? What happened ?

134 Continued 134

As the FIREMEN drag him out of the room, they crush KEVIN's chequerboard lying half folded on the floor. On the chequerboard rests a toy tank, laser gun and a variety of toy cowboys, knights and archers. It looks to be a close copy of the Great Hall.

135 EXT. KEVIN'S HOUSE DAWN 135

The FIREMAN carries KEVIN out, passing his distraught PARENTS who stand outside in the half-light of dawn in dressing gowns and curlers - he holding a digital clock, timer, alarm and music centre with wires trailing in one hand.

MOTHER
(almost hysterically)
I've got to save it, Trevor....!

FATHER
(holding her back)
Don't be a fool, Diane.

MOTHER
I'm going in for the toaster...!

She makes to push into the smoking house, but he holds her back. At the truck the FIREMAN sets KEVIN down.

FIREMAN
You're alright, now ?

KEVIN double-takes. There's something about the FIREMAN.

KEVIN
Yes, I think so ... Thank you. I -

At the door of the house, FIREMEN are clearing up, carrying rolled-up hoses out.

KEVIN's MOTHER is busy shouting at her husband who is trying to restrain her.

MOTHER
If you were half a man you'd have gone in there and saved the blender ...

ANOTHER FIREMAN
(interrupting them)
This is what started it ... left the Sunday joint cooking all night ...

He is holding an ultra-modern micro-wave oven from which black smoke is issuing.

Back to KEVIN, who looks down; in sudden amazement he feels something in his pocket. Reaching down he brings out a Polaroid; it's AGAMEMNON, and AGAMEMNON looks exactly like the Fireman who just saved him. He looks up in amazement. Behind him sounds of fire engines packing up. Yes ... and to prove it ... as the door slams, SEAN CONNERY winks down at him.

KEVIN's jaw drops. He turns, looks back again at the photo.

MOTHER
(Surveying what looks like highly over-done piece of beef top-side smoking in her oven)
Sunday joint ? It's Thursday!

FATHER
Well, I haven't touched it ...

MOTHER
<u>Someone</u> put it on ....

KEVIN looks at his parents.

MOTHER
If you'd bought the de-luxe model this wouldn't have happened.

KEVIN registers, a look of horror crossed his cheap young features.

FATHER
There was no meat in there last night.

MOTHER
(cross at his stubborness)
Well what do you think this is then?

She opens the oven. KEVIN now sees clearly what he had suspected all along. In there is nothing less than a piece of the most dangerous substance known to man - It is the missing piece of EVIL !

KEVIN
Mum! Mum!

FATHER
(reaching into the oven)
Let me see.

KEVIN
No ... Dad ... don't

But as DAD reaches in there is a polite but definite explosion of the sort EVIL was always doling out, and MUM and DAD are reduced to two simmering piles on the front lawn.

KEVIN
Mum? ....Dad?

THE END
or is it....?

Katherine Helmond tries her head on.

Peter Vaughan and Terry Gilliam wait for the unit dentist.

Henley Regatta 1902.
The early heats.

Mike Edmonds and yacht at Cannes.

A party in the men's showers.

Cannibals visit the set.
The gang are presented.

John and Cynthia Cleese meet one of the backers.

George Harrison and Denis O'Brien discuss the size of their credits.

Sir Ralph Richardson tells the producers his fee.

Sir Ralph Richardson and Terry Gilliam discuss the size of <u>their</u> credits.

Disco Night on the set. David Warner and patrons

The director hears he has to stay on the film.

SAATCHI & SAATCHI TRY NEW IMAGE FOR MRS. THATCHER.

Michael Palin and Shelley Duvall forget their lines.

Kevin sprinkles Magic Powder on Shelley Duvall.

Malcolm, Katherine and Mike discuss a medical problem.

Agamemnon and Clytemnestra discuss single sex schooling.

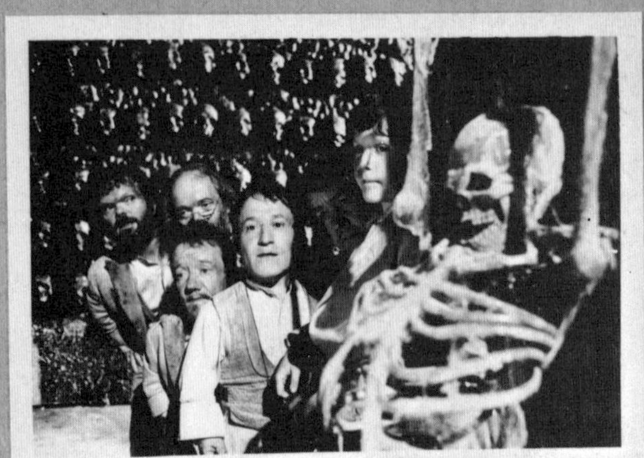

David and the gang meet other actors who have worked with Terry Gilliam.

Barbra Streisand Impersonati
1st round winners

TIME BANDITS

by Terry Gilliam and Michael Palin

Producer and Director: Terry Gilliam   Music: George Harrison
Executive Producers: George Harrison and Denis O'Brien
Associate Producer: Neville C. Thompson   Editor: Julian Doyle
Director of Photography: Peter Biziou   Production Designer: Milly Burns
Costume Designer: Jim Acheson   Costume Advisor: Hazel Cote
Hairdresser/Make-up: Maggie Weston and Elaine Carew
Art Director: Norman Garwood

Starring

Robin Hood .... John Cleese
King Agamemnon .... Sean Connery
Pansy .... Shelley Duvall
Mrs. Ogre .... Katherine Helmond
Napoleon .... Ian Holm
Vincent .... Michael Palin
Supreme Being .... Ralph Richardson
Ogre .... Peter Vaughan
Evil Genius .... David Warner

with

Randall .... David Rappaport
Fidgit .... Kenny Baker
Wally .... Jack Purvis
Og .... Mike Edmonds
Strutter .... Malcolm Dixon
Vermin .... Tiny Ross
Kevin .... Craig Warnock

Also appearing

Lucien .... Terence Bayler
Compere .... Jim Broadbent
Baxi Brazilia II .... Martin Carroll
Robber Leader .... Derrick O'Connor
Kenvin's Father .... David Daker
Robert .... Derek Deadman
Bullheaded Warrior .... Winston Dennis
Greek Warrior .... Del Baker
Beryl .... Myrtle Devenish
Kenvin's Mother .... Sheila Fearn
Cartwright .... Roger Frost
Myrtle .... Joan Hickson
The Great Rumbozo .... John Hughman
Clytemnestra .... Juliette James
Puppeteer .... David Leland
Neguy .... Preston Lockwood
Giant .... Ian Muir
Theatre Manager .... Charles McKeown
Robber 2 .... Declan Mullholland
Robber 3 .... Neil McCarthy
Fireman .... Andrew McLachlan
Horseflesh .... Marcus Powell
Benson .... Jerold Wells
1st Refugee .... Leon Lissek
Reginald .... John Young

Camera Operator .... David Garfath
Camera Focus...................... Robert Stilwell
Clapper Loader .... Simon Fulford
Camera Grip .... Freddie Fry

2nd Unit Cameraman ....Julian Doyle
2nd Unit Focus ....Brian Herlihy
2nd Unit Grip .... Tony Andrews

Casting Director ....Irene Lamb

Production Manager .... Graham Ford
Location Manager...............Patrick Cassavetti
1st Assistant Director .... Simon Hinkly
2nd Assistant Director ....Guy Travers
Production Assistant .... Linda Bruce
Producer's Assistant................. Rachel Neale
3rd Assistant Director................Mark Cooper
3rd Assistant Director............ Chris Thompson
Runner ....Steve Parker

Assistant Art Director................ Celia Barnett
Construction Manager ....Peter Verard
Modelmaker.......................... Val Charlton
Assistant Model Makers .... Carol de Jong
Jean Ramsey

Production Buyer.................. Karen Brookes
Draughtsman ....Steven Cooper

Make-up Artist .... Sue Frear

Assistant Costume Designer ..... T. Stephen Miles
Wardrobe Mistress .... Dorothea Smylie
Wardrobe Assistants ....Gilly Hebden
Tony Williams

Sound Mixer ....Garth Marshall
Boom Operator..........................Bob Doyle
Sound Maintenance .... Philip Chubb

Assistant Editor ....Rodney Glenn

Special Effects Senior Technician.................. John Bunker
Pyrotechnics..........................Chris Verner
Andy Thompson

Special Effects Modellers ....Chris Overs
Lewis Coleman
Special Effects Runner .... Chris Ostwald

Property Master........................Peter Grant
S/By Prop.............................. John Cole
S/By Prop...........................Dave Newton
Dressing Prop ....Ray Perry
Prop Dresser .... Steve Wheeler
Drapes................................Ron Cowen

Supervising C/H Carpenter............... Len Day
C/H Carpenter...................... Micky Fisher
C/H Plasterer..........................Eric Nash
C/H Painter .... John Davey
C/H Rigger .... Dave Everall

S/By Carpenter ....Craig Hillier
S/By Painter .... Graham Bullock
Alan Grenham
S/By Stagehand..................... Douglas Cox
S/By Rigger........................ Dave Wiggins

Gaffer Spark .... Roy Rodhouse
Gaffer .... Reg Parsons
Best Boy............................. Chuck Finch
Electrician........................ Stuart Monteith
Electrician............................ Tug Wilson

Drivers .... Brian Brookner
Tony Hocking

Chaperone........................ Yvette Warnock

Tutor ....Shirley Draffan
Fight Arranger .... Peter Brayham

Horseman ....Brain Bowes

Production Accountant .... Brian Bailey
Assistant Accountants ....Raymond Parsons
Michael Yell
Accounts Secretary ....Geraldine Dunn

Stillsman ....Clive Coote

Choreographer .... Tom Jobe